RECIPES · CULTURE · STORIES

# busaba

## BANGKOK · THAI
## COOKBOOK

sphere

BANGKOK · THAI

First published in Great Britain in 2018 by Sphere

A CIP catalogue record for this book is available from
the British Library.

ISBN 978-0-7515-7185-1

Printed and bound in China

10 9 8 7 6 5 4 3 2

Book creation and design by Harris + Wilson Ltd

**Managing Editor:** Judy Barratt
**Art Director:** Manisha Patel
**Recipe Developers:** Nicola Graimes, Tamas Khan,
Winston Matthews and Jude Krit Sangsida
**Recipe Photographer:** Dave Brown @ Ape Inc.

**Sphere**
An imprint of
Little, Brown Book Group, Carmelite House,
50 Victoria Embankment, London EC4Y 0DZ

An Hachette UK Company
www.hachette.co.uk
www.littlebrown.co.uk

**NOTES ON THE RECIPES**
*Unless otherwise specified, use:*
Medium free-range or organic eggs
Fresh herbs
Medium vegetables
Full-fat dairy products
Unwaxed citrus fruits
Organic, free-range meat
Fish from sustainable sources

Oven temperatures are for a fan-assisted oven.
Use metric or imperial measurements in your cooking,
not a mixture of both.

Shop-bought sauces, condiments and jams may include
allergens. Please always check the labels – and all your
ingredients – before using if you are cooking for someone
with allergies.

All the information in this book is correct to the best of
our knowledge. If there are any errors or omissions, we
will, if notified, make corrections in any future editions.

# CONTENTS

# GAN GIN GAN YUU
## AS YOU EAT, SO YOU ARE

From the first day it was founded, Busaba Bangkok Thai has been about discovery and experience. Our family of restaurants is where you'll find our love of Thai food and Thai culture colliding to create our unique take on what a modern Thai restaurant should offer – innovative and fresh, high-quality Thai dishes in bold Bangkok-influenced surroundings.

Our obsession with fantastic food is guided by a Thai expression *gan gin gan yuu*, which means 'as you eat, so you are'. Through this philosophy, we realize that, as people, we are defined by the food we eat. If we eat healthily, we are healthy; if we eat in balance, we are in balance. This philosophy inspires everything we do at Busaba, from the quality of our ingredients (including our attention to detail when we choose who and where to source our food), through training our chefs and preparing our recipes, to the presentation of our dishes as they arrive at the table for our guests.

In the Busaba family, we also take to heart another Thai philosophy: *namjai*, which translated literally means 'water of the heart'. In Thai culture it means taking pleasure in making sacrifices for friends, and extending hospitality and generosity to strangers, who are simply those who are friends in waiting. The spirit of *namjai* is in everything we do. Fundamentally, kindness, thoughtfulness, gentle style and humble confidence are the bedrock for our true nature. It is always with respect for *namjai* that we bring the flavours, the aromas and the buzz of Bangkok to life in each of our restaurants.

We hope you enjoy creating the dishes in this book and, more importantly, we hope that you, too, adopt the spirit of *namjai* as you do so. If you add your own heart, style and confidence to your cooking, every mouthful becomes nourishment not only for your body, but also for your soul – and for the body and soul of anyone who dines with you. As you eat, so you are.

*Khop khun* (simply, thank you),
The Busaba Team

# THE BUSABA STORY

The first Busaba Eathai restaurant (our original name) opened in 1999 on Wardour Street in Soho, London. Now a thriving social hub, at that time Wardour Street was home to only three eateries. Nonetheless, Alan Yau, Busaba's founder, had a vision to create a new style of Thai restaurant, reflecting Buddhist values and Thai culture that were married to inspiring food and modern design, and place it in London's social heartland.

Busaba was to be a journey of discovery: its location, discrete signage, and dark, stylish interior were all consciously picked to draw in customers who wanted to try something different. The food, inspired by the immediacy and freshness of Thailand's street-food culture, intended to stretch visitors' impression of typical Thai fare beyond the ubiquitous green curry. Furthermore, the setting gathered its guests around large, communal square tables, drawing on the Thai ethos that eating should be a shared experience, where families, friends and strangers alike gather to enjoy and to nourish.

Word soon spread. The cultural and culinary authenticity of the fresh, quality ingredients served up at Busaba before long began to attract a cool crowd of trendy foodies, who wanted to experience for themselves this secret gem.

Four years after the opening of that first restaurant in the heart of Soho, a second Busaba emerged, not too far away in Bloomsbury, London. Since then, the name Busaba has become synonymous with the simple flavours and freshness of authentic Thai food. Each restaurant (there are now many more) has its own unique personality that respectfully connects it to its surroundings. In keeping with that initial vision, Busaba looks for harmony in its locations, holding fast to the Buddhist notion that happiness comes when we allow ourselves to flow with time and space rather than against it, in everything we do.

busaba

BANGKOK · THAI

# SOOKJAI
## HAPPY HEART

### SOOKJAI

At the heart of everything Busaba stands for, and has done since its opening, is the culture of *sookjai*, meaning 'happy heart'. We like to think that in the pursuit of *sookjai*, we can offer our guests an escape, a sanctuary from the chaos and stress of everyday life. Coupled with our underlying principle of *namjai* (see page 9), we know that however the Busaba family changes and grows (as all families must), living and working by *sookjai* enables us to remain steadfast to our guiding values. We don't just say these things, though. We believe them, and we ensure that every Busaba restaurant is blessed and attuned to the philosophies we claim to uphold.

### THE MONK'S BLESSING FOR OUR SPACE

Before we open a new restaurant, we invite a Buddhist monk to bless the site, encouraging good fortune both for the restaurant and those who work in it, and also for all our visitors. We ask for the spirits of those who have occupied the space before us to allow us to share their home in harmony.

### DAILY RITUAL

In the practice of Buddhism, ritual is an important part of everyday life. Through reverence for the Buddha, Buddhists believe that we can move one step closer to the goal of Enlightenment – release from the cycle of life, death and rebirth into the blissful state of Nirvana. When we opened our first restaurant in 1999, we adopted several rituals and traditions that we believe align our fortunes across our whole business and harmonize our guests' experience and enjoyment when they come to visit.

### THREE OFFERINGS TO BUDDHA

Every day we pay our respects to the Buddha, whose image welcomes our guests at each of our restaurants. We place his image on a stand as high as possible. Every day before noon, we present the Buddha with fresh fruit and water, and a small bowl of food, in order to honour and nourish him and in doing so progress on our path to Enlightenment. Then, we perform three daily rituals:

The lighting of the candles This represents the light of the Buddha's teachings, which drive away the darkness of ignorance.

The lighting of the incense Three incense sticks represent each of the three Buddhist gems: Buddha himself, the Dharma (Buddha's teaching) and Sangha (the Buddha's founding community of monks).

The presentation of a bowl of floating flowers Our colourful gerberas symbolize impermanence, reminding us to live in the present moment.

In addition, at the beginning and the end of each day, we sound a gong, to represent the start of work and start of rest, respectively.

### THE AUSPICES OF THE 'LUCKY LADY'

You'll often see a golden lucky lady set high up in our restaurants. She is Nang Kwak (the Buddhist spirit of good fortune), who is depicted holding a pot of treasure, which represents wealth and abundance. Traditional Thai legend claims that she saved local villagers from an evil giant, and they were so grateful they showered her with rewards.

### SYNERGY IN THE THREE CLOCKS

Each section in our restaurants has its own feature clock, to bring synergy to our teams.

The red clock Red represents luck, so we place this clock in our main restaurant to bring good fortune to our front-of-house staff and our customers.

The white clock Representing cleanliness, purity and innocence, a white clock is in each kitchen.

The gold clock Chosen to represent the wisdom of the Buddha, a gold clock is in each restaurant office.

# THE CULTURE OF THAI FOOD

Intriguing, diverse, surprising and powerful, Thai cooking is an uncompromising fusion of regional cooking and cultural identity. It is at once unapologetically distinctive and characteristically open-hearted (in the nature of Thai culture itself), welcoming influences not just from its neighbours in Asia (notably Laos, Cambodia, Malaysia and a little further afield, China and India), but from around the world, too. As a result, Thai food is a leading world cuisine that both is unique and blends seamlessly with the identity of others.

The aim of Thai cooking is simple: good flavour. However, in their practice, Thai cooking and eating are packed with Buddhist notions and ideals. The experience of eating Thai is not just about the food itself, but about the way in which we eat it, too.

## MEALS FOR SHARING

The strong community spirit in Thailand and even stronger family bonds mean that meals are seen predominantly as occasions for sharing. A Thai family meal is, typically, a variety of dishes placed in the centre of the table for everyone to help themselves. There aren't 'courses' in the way we think of them in the West. A typical Thai meal might include – at the same time – a soup, a fried dish, steamed vegetables, at least one curry dish, and a variety of sauces and condiments. Each person will

serve him- or herself, and maybe others, from the array of aromatic and colourful dishes on the table, using a serving spoon (*chon klang*). Most Thais eat steamed rice, ladled out by the host – some Thais have even been known to say that without rice, there is no meal at all.

## BEAUTIFUL FOOD IN BEAUTIFUL WAYS

Presentation of food is incredibly important in Thailand. Thais instinctively understand that our hunger – and so our digestion and ultimate satisfaction – begins with what we see on our plates, even before we fill our bellies.

Thai chefs can spend hours creating delicate and intricate carvings from fruits and vegetables to accompany a meal they are preparing. These beautiful carvings are

often used for food offerings to monks, when entertaining guests at weddings, and as part of cultural displays for visitors to Thailand. In restaurants, bright red and green chilli slices, or delicate fresh flowers in vibrant colours, make our eyes pop moments before our tongues follow suit.

## STREET-FOOD CULTURE

In the West, we tend not to graze on food, but in Thailand snacking is a cultural norm. There is scarcely a Thai dish that is not sold by a street vendor or at a market. In Thailand, people gather at communal market tables to eat, and it's not unusual to see someone carrying whole meals neatly packaged in containers and bags to share at work or at home with colleagues, friends and family.

## EAT LIKE A THAI

First and foremost, let's talk cutlery. Although you will find chopsticks in Thailand (and, for that matter, in Busaba) most Thais do not use them and prefer, instead, to use a fork and a spoon (more often than a fork and a knife). The adoption of chopsticks, when they appear, is largely because of the Chinese custom of using them to eat noodles, which, of course, originated in China (see page 18).

Second, be open-minded about when you eat what. Thais don't really have specific dishes for breakfast, lunch and dinner. Eat what you fancy when you fancy it, rather than thinking a certain food is for a certain time of day. If you want to eat fried rice for breakfast and soup for dinner, or vice versa, that's truly in the spirit of Thai eating culture.

Finally, don't waste food. Thai people believe it is bad luck to throw food away. When eating, Thais avoid combining different dishes on their plates, but rather, they sample one dish at a time and take only what they need. Any leftovers are reborn into something new and equally delicious.

# THE PRINCIPLES OF THAI COOKING

Thailand has always been a land of plenty. Fertile soils and a tropical climate give rise to amazing fresh produce, and provide a terrain on which livestock can thrive. Seas and rivers brim with fish – tilapia, catfish, sea and river prawns, and oysters among them. With such abundance, is it any wonder, then, that Thailand has provided us with such a culinary cornucopia? Because of the amazing climate, many ingredients found in Thai food go quickly from 'field to feast', giving that characteristic freshness. In Thai cuisine, cooking is just about as in-the-moment as it can be.

## WORLDWIDE INFLUENCE

In a sense, the rules of Thai cooking are really very flexible. After all, modern Thai cuisine is steeped both in the country's ancient history and in its ability to absorb and adapt the best ingredients, foods, flavourings and techniques from elsewhere.

At the heart of Thai cooking lie the culinary traditions of ancient Siam (the name for Thailand until 1939): simple grilled, steamed or stewed meat and fish dishes aromatically flavoured with the native herbs (Thai basil and lemongrass, for example). Add rice and, across the centuries, Thailand has been able to serve up balanced, flavourful meals from its own soils and waters.

Yet, Thailand has also become a melting pot of the best from the rest of the world. As the Chinese colonized the countries bordering Thailand, so they brought with them noodles, and new cooking techniques, most notably the stir-fry. Inevitably, these influences crept over the border into Thailand itself: when the Chinese introduced the wok, the Thais made *pad Thai*, now arguably Thailand's most famous dish. And what of chilli? Who can imagine a Thai curry without it? But the chilli is not native to Thailand: it was the Portuguese who brought it in the 17th century, having first discovered it in South America. Meanwhile, from India, the Thais adopted the notion of using dried spices – cardamom and cumin among them. The result is a clear culinary identity that, on close inspection, is in fact as much food fusion as you might find in the coolest modern restaurants in Bangkok today.

But what does all this mean when it comes to cooking at home, in our own kitchens? It means that the first principle of Thai cooking is to make like Thai chefs from throughout history: be open-hearted when you cook. Take the recipes and don't be afraid to adapt and experiment, using the best ingredients and favourite flavours you have found throughout your own culinary adventures. If you like things especially hot, add more chilli; if you like things creamy, add coconut milk. The Thai feast includes sides of sauces and dips, allowing diners to add and flavour specifically according to their own likes and dislikes. In addition, a squeeze of lime and a sprinkling of Thai basil or coriander, or a scattering of fresh mango remind us that freshness – field to feast – is key. There is nothing cloying about Thai food.

## BALANCING THE FLAVOUR PROFILES

Human beings are said to be able to identify six flavour profiles: salty, sweet, sour, spicy, bitter and umami (savoury). Of these, the first four form the foundation of Thai cooking. If you can successfully combine these flavours in the right quantities and with the right balance, the harmony is said to be perfectly satisfying for the senses as well as the palate.

To that end, know that sour flavours will bring out salty flavours in other ingredients; salty flavours (often through the addition of fish sauce in Thai cooking, rather than salt itself) will bring out sweetness; and sweet and sour flavours will balance spiciness (and vice versa).

# THAI COOKING REGION BY REGION

Influences from other parts of the world, and from Thailand's neighbouring countries (see page 14) are only part of the culinary story. At more than 510,000km² (over twice the land area of the UK), Thailand's land mass provides varied terrain, from the mountainous north to the peninsula in the south. Inevitably, this means that across the country each geographical region has its own distinctive cuisine that reflects its specific agriculture and climate. The country is divided roughly into the regions of northern, northeastern, central and southern Thailand.

## NORTHERN THAILAND

Bordering Myanmar (formerly Burma) and Laos, northern Thailand is a cool, mountainous region, where vegetables grow in abundance. Roots and bitter herbs have a strong presence, which means that many sour and bitter flavours dominate the local dishes here, especially the soups. Braising and grilling are popular cooking techniques for northern dishes, and rice is generally sticky (known as 'glutinous', containing a single starchy carbohydrate that gives it its stickiness), rather than the steamed looser grains of white rice that you'll find elsewhere in the country. Sticky rice is perfect for eating without cutlery – for the true northern Thai experience roll it into balls with your hands and dip the balls into chilli sauce or use them to mop up curry juices.

Whereas to many Westerners coconut milk seems like a staple ingredient in Thai food, in northern Thailand it rarely (although there are exceptions) makes an appearance. The temperate climate means that coconuts don't grow here, so dishes tend to be based on sauces made using a base of water or broth. As a result, the curries are generally thinner and less sweet than you might commonly find elsewhere in the country.

Thanks to influences from its bordering countries and, of course, the movement of the Chinese, Thailand's northern provinces brim with different noodle dishes. In Chiang Mai, Thailand's most significant northern city, famous for its many beautiful temples, most popular of all are *khao soi* egg noodles, which some say originate from the noodle dishes of neighbouring Myanmar.

Whereas fish is hugely popular in other regions of Thailand, in the landlocked north pork is the protein of choice. Pork sausages are a speciality: the meat is ground with dried chillies, garlic, shallots and lemongrass to produce a deliciously aromatic and spicy red sausage.

## NORTHEASTERN THAILAND

A vast plateau, flanked by the Mekong River, northeastern Thailand (also known as Isaan) has a dry, hot climate. The people of northeastern Thailand are, in the main, ethnically Lao, with a smaller number originating from Khmer. Unsurprisingly, then, this has a heavy bearing on the types of dish produced here.

Furthermore, fuel supply (in the form of wood) is scarce here compared with other parts of Thailand, which means fresh salads and cured meats and fish are popular. It's fairly common to see vendors selling soups made with preserved fish. Dishes tend to be spicy and herby. The layers of flavour are awesome, but the preparation is often relatively simple: grilling and boiling being the preferred methods of cooking. As in northern Thailand, sticky rice is the preferred carbohydrate.

Perhaps the most iconic dish of the region, however, is *som tam* – a salad in which green papaya is pounded in a mortar with lime juice, garlic and fish sauce and a number of other ingredients, such as dried shrimp, cherry tomatoes and roasted peanuts. The result is a hot, spicy, tangy salad that

now appears in restaurants all over Thailand. We've included our own version of this classic on page 202.

There are two other northeastern Thai dishes that deserve special mention. The first is *kai yang* or grilled chicken. For this dish, the chicken is rubbed with a marinade of garlic, coriander root, black pepper and fish sauce, and is then slowly cooked over hot charcoal, before being served with a variety of dips, and – of course – sticky rice (this dish has inspired our char-grilled chicken recipe on page 159). The second is the larb (see page 100). Originating from Laos, the larb is very much now part of northeastern Thai cuisine – minced meat (usually pork), flavoured with chilli, lime and herbs in a tangy 'salad', now often served in a leaf (such as a lettuce leaf) cup, although traditionally with (you guessed it) sticky rice.

## CENTRAL THAILAND

A large delta expanse, with rich, fertile soil and intersected by the Chao Phraya River, the land of central Thailand is dominated by paddy rice fields, orchards and vegetable gardens. In many ways, we might think of this region as the centre of Thai culture and the home of the quintessential Thai people. The language spoken here is how we think of classic Thai (other regions, particularly in the north, each have a distinct dialect of their own).

Many of the dishes familiar to Westerners originate from the central Thai region. Among them are the famous hot-and-sour *tom yam* soup (see page 80), and the possibly even more famous Thai green curry (*kaeng khieo wan*; see page 116). Jasmine rice is cultivated here.

Flavours in this region's food tend to be highly complex, dominated by spicy and salty, and often balanced with the tangy sourness of the lime that grows in abundance. The primary meats are chicken, duck and pork, while prawns and freshwater fish are also readily available.

## SOUTHERN THAILAND

Sandwiched between the Andaman Sea on one side and the Gulf of Thailand on the other, the peninsula that forms southern Thailand is heavily Malay in ethnicity (and it forms the only land route from mainland Asia to Malaysia and Singapore). Here, the scenery and culture is dramatically different to the rest of Thailand – beaches lapped by crystal-clear waters, river plains, cliffs that rise starkly from the sea, and mountains all feature along this strip of land.

The region is blessed with coconut groves (and rice fields) aplenty, which means that coconut milk, cream and oil play a leading role in the food. For example, the south produces curries that are very thick and rich and creamy. Cashew nuts and pineapple also grow in great quantities and feature heavily in the local dishes.

Unsurprisingly, perhaps, seafood is huge in southern Thai cuisine. Prawns, lobsters, crabs, scallops, oysters, squid and mackerel are simply steamed or fried, or cooked more exotically in a clay pot (a sort of Thai version of the Moroccan tagine) with noodles.

The hot sun of the south is handy for drying foods, and in the spirit of no waste (see page 15), if something isn't eaten there and then it's sun-dried for another time. Sun-drying gives us shrimp paste, a key ingredient in many southern relishes.

Interestingly, southern Thailand is home to many of the country's Muslims (Thailand's largest religious minority), particularly in the provinces closest to Malaysia, where trade routes from the Islamic world brought many spices. Even this far south, the influences of Indian and Chinese cooking peep through. For example, fresh turmeric, brought originally by Indian merchants to the region, turns many southern curries a distinctive yellow.

In a country famous for its spicy food, the south is where you'll find Thai cooking at its most fiery. Southerners like their food fantastically chilli-hot, sour and salty – but it's that heat that really makes their food sing.

# BANGKOK THAI

In central Thailand, on the Chao Phraya River delta, lies Bangkok, dominating not just the region, but Thailand's entire cultural landscape. So many capital cities in the world are a melting pot of all walks of life, art and vibe, but somehow Bangkok manages to combine it all with special vibrancy that is uniquely Thai – and uniquely Bangkokian. Even the street art shouts energy – bold lines, geometric patterns and bright colours seem to light up walls at every turn.

That melting pot is never more apparent than in Bangkok's food scene. When work has been scarce elsewhere in Thailand, particularly in the north, Thais have flocked in their thousands to their capital city, the economic centre of their country, bringing with them not just their regional customs and culture, but their local cuisines, too. The result is unrivalled variety, representing the whole of Thailand – sticky rice and delicate jasmine rice; fragrant pork balls and flaky white fish steamed in banana leaves; creamy coconut-based green curry and stock-based jungle curry. Specialities from all over Thailand are brought together in the markets and in the restaurants of Bangkok.

This is a city not only of variety but also of foodie extremes. On the one hand, hawkers spend all day and night cooking up the very best in the world's street food (international-award-winning street food, no less). Ease your way down the city's narrow

market aisles – brushing unavoidably against the hundreds of Thai office workers grabbing their breakfast, lunch or evening meal – to find everything from spicy meat curries or sweet-and-sour fish served with noodles to delicate omelette parcels filled with the freshest, most delicious seafood (crab is a favourite; see page 70). Even the rivers and canals of the city's floating markets are thick with the aromas of freshly grilled satay, fragrant stir-fries and bananas caramelizing in their skins – among so much more.

On the other hand, Bangkok is home to sophisticated air-conditioned restaurants serving not just Thai food, but also some of the rest of the world's most exquisite fine dining. These present an eclectic mixture of cuisines as diverse as Indian and French, all presented in tranquil surroundings brought gently to life with the hushed murmur of relaxed diners.

In recent years, the Thai government has begun systematic regulation of food vendors on the city's streets. It seems inconceivable that in this thriving, buzzing city, where locals and tourists, office workers and market traders, old and young, rich and poor come together to eat in the true spirit of communal living and sharing, the culture of street food could ever be anything but everywhere. Food markets and canal and street vendors are the lifeblood of Bangkok. Despite this bureaucratic clean-up, a visit to any of the many markets in the city continues to bring a baffling treat for the

senses, with what seems almost every stall and stand offering some culinary delight to sample or take home for supper.

In the restaurants, more than the markets, classic Thai meets world cuisine. You'd be wrong if you thought that fusion was the province of the West – in Bangkok, Thai dishes are blended not only with traditional fare from other Far Eastern countries, but with Western food, too. After all, how else would we enjoy a Thai burger (see page 163)?

Of course, it's not just the city's food that inspires what we do at Busaba. Bangkok is equally famed for its vibrant nightlife. Here, the cocktail is king – with rum and gin being the spirits of choice. In fact, gin has seen something of a heyday in recent times with gin bars arriving on the scene in the coolest up-and-coming parts of town. Often, the best bars – whatever cocktails they're serving – lie behind heavy wooden doors with discreet signage, or underground in opulent, dimly lit surroundings. Some of these establishments feel more like the speakeasies of 1920s America than the more stereotypical Bangkok bar you might

imagine. In contrast, the city's many sky bars – neon-lit rooftops alive with music and social buzz (and those crowding at the precipitous edge to get the best nighttime views of the city) – feel far more extravagant. All together, the bars remind us that Bangkok is a city that somehow manages to blend the ancient Buddhist concepts of no-self and asceticism with a nightlife that literally (in the case of its cocktails) overflows with decadence – without the one feeling in any way at odds with the other.

It's all these many faces of frenetic, unique, incredible Bangkok that we try to capture in our restaurants. You can sit at a table with friends (both those known and – in the spirit of *namjai* – those yet-to-know) to eat delicious food inspired by the markets and restaurants of the city; or, you can choose a cosy corner to enjoy a quiet meal with those closest to you, watched over by our Buddha, who silently welcomes and blesses you. The wall art is straight from the streets of the city; at the bar, our cocktails immediately transport you to the buzzing nightlife of what surely must be one of the coolest places on Earth.

# USING OUR BOOK

We have divided the book into five main chapters, each broken down into subsections according to main cooking styles. You can mix and match the recipes in a sharing feast that covers all or some of the savoury chapters, or choose certain dishes to create a more Western-style meal, comprising a starter and a main, and then a dessert from the Sweet chapter. Each subsection opens with some key information about the recipes and some tips from our 'school of wok' cookery classes, which we provide for all our chefs when they join the restaurant team, under the guidance of our Head Chef and Development Chef. At the end of the book you'll find a supplementary chapter of pastes, sauces and sides, and 'Thai larder', which explains key ingredients that we use throughout the recipes and that are the staples of traditional Thai cooking.

## A NOTE ON CHILLI HEAT

At the top of each recipe we've given an indication of the chilli heat you can expect in the finished dish (see key, right). Feel free to experiment with the amount of chilli you use, because every palate and every chilli is unique and we can only really give you a rough guide as to what the finished dish will feel like on your tongue. Other ingredients may enhance or temper the heat, too – for example, curries made using coconut milk will soften the intensity of the heat in the chillies, as will those that include sweet foods, such as sweet potato.

## A NOTE ON RICE

Archaeologists suggest that rice has been growing in Thailand since prehistoric times. It is an essential part of not only Thai culture, but the Thai economy, too. To Westerners, the rice at a Thai meal is the side, but in Thailand rice takes centre stage. Sometimes it's obvious when a dish needs rice – to soak up a sauce or provide starch, for example. But

The following symbols are used, as relevant, throughout the recipes.

- **v** suitable for vegetarians
- **vg** suitable for vegans
- **gf** gluten-free
- **n** contains tree nuts, peanuts or coconut
- slight tingle
- nice and spicy
- hot stuff

Note that many (but not all) recipes can be made gluten-free by substituting certified gluten-free versions of regular ingredients, such as soy sauce, oyster sauce, and stock.

if you truly want to cook and eat the Thai way, remember that ideally rice appears at every meal, regardless of any apparent 'need' for it. Our method for cooking perfect jasmine rice appears on page 259, as does the recipe for flavoured coconut rice; while fried-rice dishes (see pages 106–111) can just as easily make complete meals on their own. Present your rice to the table with as much delight and pride as you do the other dishes in your feast. If your guests wonder why, tell them that the Rice Goddess, Mae Phosop, is an incarnation of Nang Kwak (see page 13), the goddess of good fortune – and in the spirit of Busaba it's your duty to honour her.

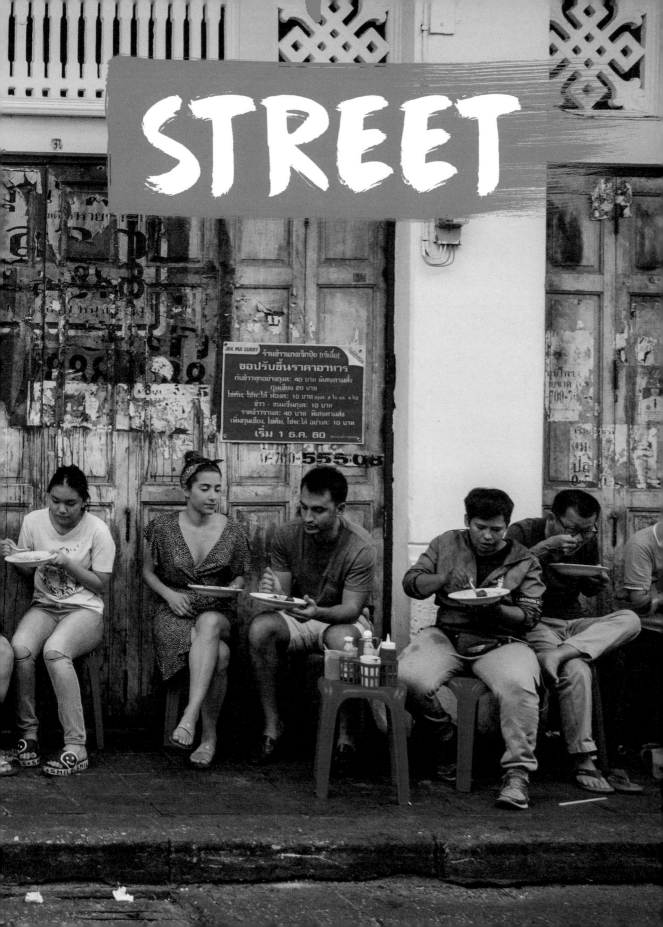

STREET

# SMALL PLATES

Most of the recipes in this chapter are street foods, reminiscent of the snacks and small bites sold from market stalls, street carts, hawkers and, despite the name 'street', river boats throughout Bangkok (and elsewhere in Thailand). Despite regulatory changes controlling the sale of street food in Bangkok, the city remains the outside dining capital of the world and its reputation holds fast.

Generally, small bites are not made at home, instead they are eaten on the go or at a table set up by the street vendor. These are casual dishes to be eaten any time of the day, morning, noon or night, whenever hunger strikes.

Anyone who wanders the bustling street markets of Bangkok cannot fail to be impressed by the vast array of dishes that are on offer. We've given you a good taster of them in this chapter. Admittedly, we've avoided any deep-fried insects, but you'll find so much else – from stuffed omelettes, rice paper rolls, and dumplings to succulent skewers, crisp golden fishcakes, fritters and our favourite, sticky chicken wings with our special sauce. Many show the culinary influence of Thailand's neighbours – Vietnamese-style steamed buns and Chinese spring rolls, for example.

Although appetizers aren't traditionally a part of a Thai meal – dishes tend to be served all together – any of these small plates would make a great starter. Or, try them as a meal in their own right, perhaps with a side dish of salad or stir-fried veg.

Street foods can be char-grilled, steamed or stir-fried, but in Thailand deep-fried is perhaps the most popular way to cook them. Made correctly, deep-fried foods should be deliciously crisp and golden, not greasy or soggy. Here are some of our top tips for getting that just right.

First, if you don't have a deep-fat fryer, a wok is a perfectly suitable alternative. In fact, because of the large surface area in a wok, you'll need less oil, which is a bonus. Do use a wok stand if your pan has a rounded base to keep it stable, though. It's also key to use the right type of oil: vegetable, rapeseed or groundnut are all good as they have a mild flavour and a high smoking point. And make sure you heat the oil to the right temperature. Deep-fry food in batches to avoid it sticking together and to prevent the oil temperature dropping. When the food is ready, scoop it out with a spatula, slotted spoon or mesh strainer and drain on kitchen paper to blot away any excess.

# CHICKEN SATAY

A satay is skewered grilled meat, usually served with a peanut sauce and cucumber relish. In this recipe the chicken is flavoured with fresh Thai spices, giving the street classic a distinctively Busaba twist.

**SERVES** 4
**PREP** 25 minutes, plus marinating
**COOK** 30 minutes

2 teaspoons coriander seeds or ground coriander
2 lemongrass sticks, peeled and finely chopped
1 teaspoon chopped fresh turmeric or turmeric powder
½ teaspoon salt
½ teaspoon caster sugar
2 tablespoons rapeseed oil, plus extra for brushing
125ml/4fl oz coconut milk
600g/1lb 5oz boneless, skinless chicken thighs, cut into 12 x 2cm/¾in wide strips

**FOR THE SATAY SAUCE**
4 tablespoons rapeseed oil
1½ tablespoons Red Curry Paste (see page 254), or ready-made paste
4 tablespoons palm sugar or light soft brown sugar
200ml/7fl oz coconut milk
a pinch of salt
2 tablespoons tamarind concentrate or paste
150g/5½oz unsalted roasted peanuts, ground

**FOR THE CUCUMBER RELISH**
2 tablespoons distilled white vinegar
½ teaspoon caster sugar
½ teaspoon salt
½ cucumber, deseeded and cut into 5mm/¼in dice
1 banana shallot, thinly sliced
1 large red chilli, thinly sliced

**YOU WILL ALSO NEED**
12 wooden bamboo skewers

1  If you're using coriander seeds, toast them in a dry wok or frying pan over a medium–low heat for 2 minutes, tossing occasionally, until they smell aromatic. Tip them into a pestle and mortar, or use a mini food processor or grinder, and grind to a powder. (Alternatively, use ready-ground coriander.) Remove 1 teaspoon of the ground coriander and set aside. Add the lemongrass and turmeric to the pestle and mortar with the remaining ground coriander and grind to a smooth paste. Spoon into a medium mixing bowl and stir in the salt, sugar, oil and coconut milk until combined. Add the chicken and massage in the paste until the meat is evenly coated. Cover and marinate in the fridge for at least 2 hours.

2  While the chicken is marinating, make the satay sauce. Heat the oil in a medium saucepan over a low heat. Add the red curry paste and cook for 4–5 minutes, stirring regularly, until the oil starts to separate out. Add the reserved ground coriander (see step 1) and the sugar and cook for 4–5 minutes, until darkened in colour. Increase the heat to medium and stir in 200ml/7fl oz of water, the coconut milk, salt, tamarind and finally the peanuts. Bring to the boil, then reduce the heat and simmer for 2 minutes, stirring continuously, until thickened. Set aside.

3  Soak the skewers in cold water for 30 minutes to stop them burning during cooking, then drain and pat dry on kitchen paper.

4  To make the cucumber relish, pour the vinegar into a small serving bowl and stir in the sugar and salt until dissolved. Add the cucumber, shallot and red chilli, stir, then set aside.

5  Remove the chicken from the marinade and thread a strip onto one of the skewers, then repeat to make 12 skewers in total.

6  Heat a griddle plate or pan over a high heat until very hot, then lightly brush with oil. Reduce the heat to medium and cook the chicken skewers for 4 minutes on each side, until golden and cooked through. (You may need to cook them in two batches.)

7  Just before serving, reheat the satay sauce briefly and spoon it into a small serving bowl. Arrange the skewers on a large serving plate and serve with the bowls of cucumber relish and warm satay sauce.

# GARLIC & BLACK PEPPER CHICKEN LIVERS

**The powerful taste and aroma of the garlic complements the flavours of the chicken livers in this simple Thai dish, usually served with sticky white rice and good at any time of the day (even for breakfast!).**

**SERVES** 4
**PREP** 15 minutes
**COOK** 10 minutes

450g/1lb chicken livers, trimmed
225ml/7¾fl oz vegetable oil
10 garlic cloves, finely chopped
1 teaspoon black peppercorns, cracked
4 tablespoons oyster sauce
1 teaspoon caster sugar
a pinch of dried chilli flakes
a pinch of freshly ground black pepper
salt and ground white pepper

**TO SERVE**
1 small spring onion, finely sliced
5 coriander sprigs, leaves picked
1 teaspoon fresh green peppercorns (optional)
1 lime, cut into quarters

1  Season the chicken livers with salt and white pepper.

2  Heat 175ml/6fl oz of the vegetable oil in a large wok or frying pan over a high heat. Add the chicken livers and fry for 4 minutes, turning them occasionally, until evenly browned. Remove and drain on kitchen paper, then set aside. Pour away the oil and wipe clean the wok or pan with kitchen paper.

3  Return the wok or pan to a high heat and pour in the remaining oil. Add the garlic and stir-fry for 1 minute or until light golden, taking care not to let it burn, then add the cracked peppercorns, oyster sauce and sugar.

4  Stir in the browned chicken livers, dried chilli flakes, ground black pepper and 4 tablespoons of water, then cook for 1 more minute, until warmed through. Spoon onto a serving plate and pour over the sauce.

5  Serve the chicken livers topped with spring onion, coriander leaves, green peppercorns, if using, and wedges of lime on the side.

Organ meats are found on menus – and family tables – throughout Thailand. Nose-to-tail eating and a zero-waste food philosophy are embedded in Thai culture.

# FISH LEMONGRASS SKEWERS

Galangal, garlic, chilli, shallots and lemongrass add flavour and aroma to these fish skewers. They are best cooked on a char-grill or barbecue for a lovely smoky flavour, but for ease you can griddle, fry or grill them, if you prefer. Whichever way you cook them, they are best made a couple of hours in advance, if there's time, to allow the flavours to mingle. Serve with sriracha sauce, and with wedges of lime for squeezing over.

**SERVES** 4
**PREP** 25 minutes, plus chilling
**COOK** 10–20 minutes

500g/1lb 2oz hake fillets or similar white fish fillets, pin-boned and skinned (about 450g/1lb without the skin), roughly chopped and patted dry
2.5cm/1in piece of galangal, peeled and roughly chopped
2 large garlic cloves, roughly chopped
1 large lemongrass stick, peeled and thinly sliced
3 shallots, roughly chopped
1 Thai red chilli, deseeded and chopped, plus extra to serve
a small handful coriander sprigs, leaves and stalks separated
1 teaspoon salt
½ teaspoon ground white pepper
1 heaped teaspoon cornflour
1 egg white, lightly beaten
groundnut oil, for brushing
sriracha sauce and lime wedges, to serve

**YOU WILL ALSO NEED**
12 lemongrass sticks or wooden bamboo skewers

1 Put the fish in a mini food processor and roughly mince; you may need to do this in two batches. Spoon the fish into a large mixing bowl.

2 Put the galangal, garlic, sliced lemongrass, shallots, chilli and coriander stalks in the food processor and blend to a paste. Spoon the mixture into the bowl containing the fish and season with the salt and pepper. Mix together until combined, then stir in the cornflour followed by the egg white. Cover the bowl and refrigerate for 1–2 hours to firm up.

3 Meanwhile, if using lemongrass sticks remove the outer layer of the stems. If using bamboo skewers, soak them in cold water for at least 30 minutes to stop them burning during cooking.

4 Divide the fish mixture into 12 portions, about 50g/1¾oz each. Take one portion and form it into a round patty, flatten slightly, then shape it around the top third of a lemongrass stick or bamboo skewer. Repeat with the remaining mixture to make 12 skewers in total.

5 Heat a char-grill, griddle pan or large frying pan over a high heat. Brush the fish skewers with oil and cook for 10 minutes or until golden all over and cooked through. (You may need to cook them in two batches.) Serve sprinkled with coriander leaves, a drizzle of sriracha sauce and with wedges of lime on the side.

Young, firm lemongrass stems make the perfect Thai skewer. The lemongrass plant can grow to over 1.2 metres (4 feet) tall with stems up to 1 metre (3 feet) in diameter. Quite a skewer!

# THAI SPRING ROLLS

**In Thai we call these** *por pia jay* **– delicious, fried spring rolls that work equally well with pork or prawns, or, as they do here, with vegetables.**

**MAKES** 16
**PREP** 25 minutes
**COOK** 10 minutes

100g/3½oz rice vermicelli noodles
400g/14oz Chinese leaves, thinly
 sliced
1 small carrot, finely shredded
2 spring onions, finely sliced
50g/1¾oz shiitake mushrooms,
 finely sliced
2 garlic cloves, finely chopped
½ teaspoon salt
a pinch of ground white pepper
2 tablespoons plain flour or
 cornflour
16 spring roll wrappers, defrosted
 if frozen
vegetable oil, for deep-frying
Sweet Chilli Tomato Sauce
 (see page 257) or sriracha
 sauce, to serve

1 Put the noodles in a heatproof bowl and pour over enough just-boiled water from a kettle to cover and stir well to loosen. Leave the noodles for 3–5 minutes, until softened, then drain, refresh under cold running water and place in a large mixing bowl. Add the fresh vegetables and garlic, then season with the salt and pepper. Using tongs, mix everything together until thoroughly combined, then set aside.

2 Mix together the flour or cornflour with 2 tablespoons of water to form a smooth paste – this will help to seal the spring rolls.

3 Lay a spring roll wrapper on a work surface with the corner facing you. (Keep the other wrappers covered with a clean damp cloth to stop them drying out.) Put 2 tablespoons of the filling mixture in the middle. Fold the corner nearest you over the filling, then fold over both sides, wetting them slightly so they stick. Brush the top corner with a little of the flour paste, then roll up tightly to seal. Repeat with the remaining wrappers and filling to make 16 rolls in total. Cover with a damp tea towel to stop the rolls drying out if you're not cooking them straightaway.

4 To cook, pour enough oil into a large wok (use a wok stand to keep the pan stable), saucepan or deep-fat fryer to deep-fry the spring rolls. Heat the oil to 180°C/350°F or until a cube of day-old bread turns crisp and golden in 45 seconds.

5 Add the spring rolls to the hot oil and deep-fry for 3 minutes, until crisp and golden (you may need to cook them in two batches). Remove with a slotted spatula and set aside to drain on kitchen paper.

6 To serve, place the spring rolls on a serving plate with a dish of sweet chilli tomato sauce or sriracha sauce on the side for dipping.

# STICKY & SPICY HOT BUFFALO WINGS

What could be better than deep-fried chicken wings? Answer: deep-fried chicken wings that are coated in a hot, spicy sauce! The perfect small plate in anticipation of a Thai-style feast.

**SERVES** 4
**PREP** 15 minutes
**COOK** 25 minutes

20 chicken wings, patted dry and folded at the joint to make a triangle
4 tablespoons light soy sauce
100ml/3½fl oz Sweet Chilli Sauce (see page 257) or sriracha sauce
vegetable oil, for deep-frying
1 finely sliced red chilli and 2–3 coriander sprigs, to garnish

1 Place the chicken wings in a shallow dish, pour the soy sauce over, turn the wings in the sauce until coated all over and leave to marinate for 10 minutes.

2 Meanwhile, in a small saucepan, heat the sweet chilli sauce or sriracha sauce over a medium heat for 2 minutes or until sticky and caramelized. Set aside.

3 Pour enough oil into a large wok (use a wok stand to keep the pan stable), saucepan or deep-fat fryer to deep-fry the chicken. Heat the oil to 180°C/350°F or until a cube of day-old bread turns crisp and golden in 45 seconds.

4 Drain the chicken wings and discard the soy sauce. Add a third of the chicken wings to the hot oil and deep-fry for 5 minutes, until golden brown and cooked through. Remove from the oil and set aside to dry on kitchen paper. Deep-fry the remaining wings until all are cooked.

5 To serve, reheat the chilli sauce briefly, then spoon it over the fried wings and turn them in the sauce until coated. Arrange the wings on a serving platter and garnish with the fresh chilli and coriander.

Sweet Chilli Sauce adds a fiery hit to all manner of Thai foods – from these wings to dressings, stir-fries, broths and noodle dishes. Chillies – fresh and dried – vary hugely in heat. Our Sweet Chilli Sauce recipe uses a medium-hot dried chilli combined with a hotter fresh Thai red one. If you like a hot–hot–hot sauce, you can substitute a type of chilli that ramps up the fire still further.

gf

# SON-IN-LAW EGGS

This simple deep-fried egg recipe, served with a sweet-and-sour tamarind sauce, is particularly popular with children all over Thailand. The name comes from a Thai legend in which a mother, unhappy with the way her son-in-law was treating her daughter, fried up boiled eggs as a sign of what she might do to his own body-parts if he didn't shape up!

**SERVES** 4
**PREP** 20 minutes
**COOK** 25 minutes

8 eggs
vegetable oil, for deep-frying

**FOR THE SAUCE**
3 tablespoons vegetable oil
40g/1½oz garlic cloves, finely
    chopped
40g/1½oz banana shallot, finely
    chopped
80g/2¾oz palm sugar or light soft
    brown sugar
80g/2¾oz caster sugar
150g/5½oz tamarind concentrate
    or paste
80ml/2½fl oz fish sauce
1 teaspoon potato flour
salt

**TO SERVE**
2 whole dried chillies
40g/1½oz Golden Fried Shallots
    (see page 258) or ready-made
    crispy fried shallots
3 coriander sprigs, torn

1 First, toast the dried chillies. Preheat the grill to medium and grill for 2–3 minutes, turning once, until they smell aromatic. Set aside to use later, to serve.

2 To make the sauce, heat the oil in a small saucepan over a high heat. Add the garlic and shallot and fry for 4 minutes, until golden brown. Add both types of sugar, the tamarind, fish sauce and 150ml/5fl oz of water. Reduce the heat to medium–low and simmer for 5 minutes, stirring occasionally. Mix the potato flour with 3 tablespoons of water to a smooth paste. Add to the sauce and continue to simmer, stirring, until thickened to a coating consistency.

3 Meanwhile, bring a medium saucepan of lightly salted water to the boil. Gently add the eggs and boil for about 7 minutes (less time if the eggs are on the small side). Scoop the eggs out with a slotted spoon and plunge them into a bowl of iced water. This will help to prevent a dark ring forming around the yolk and make the eggs easier to peel. Once cooled, peel the eggs.

4 Pour enough oil into a large wok (use a wok stand to keep the pan stable), saucepan or deep-fat fryer to deep-fry the eggs. Heat the oil to 180°C/350°F or until a cube of day-old bread turns crisp and golden in 45 seconds.

5 Add half of the eggs to the hot oil and deep-fry for 5 minutes or until golden brown all over. Using a slotted spoon, scoop out the eggs and drain on kitchen paper. Repeat with the second batch of eggs.

6 To serve, reheat the sauce briefly. Cut the eggs in half and arrange on a serving platter. Spoon over the sauce and sprinkle over the crispy shallots, crumble over the toasted chillies and scatter over the torn coriander sprigs.

# RICE PAPER ROLLS
# WITH STICKY PORK

**Thai street-food vendors sell various versions of these light and healthy rice paper rolls, with fillings ranging from prawn and crabstick to tofu and pork. They always come with a pot of dipping sauce for dunking.**

**MAKES** 25
**PREP** 30 minutes
**COOK** 30 minutes

50g/1¾oz rice vermicelli noodles
25 x 16cm/6¼in round rice paper
  wrappers

**FOR THE FILLING**
2 tablespoons yellow bean paste
1 Little Gem lettuce, finely
  shredded
4 spring onions, halved crossways
  and cut into long strips
7cm/2¾in piece of cucumber,
  quartered lengthways, deseeded
  and cut into thin strips
1 medium-hot red chilli, deseeded
  and cut into thin strips
300g/10½oz Slow-cooked Spiced
  Pork Belly (see page 172) or
  ready-roasted pork, shredded
25 large Thai basil leaves or regular
  basil

**FOR THE DIPPING SAUCE**
3 tablespoons Sweet Chilli Sauce
  (see page 257) or sriracha sauce
3 tablespoons lime juice

1  Put the noodles in a heatproof bowl and pour over enough just-boiled water from a kettle to cover, and stir well to loosen. Leave the noodles for 3–5 minutes, until softened, then drain, refresh under cold running water and place in a bowl.

2  Mix together all the ingredients for the dipping sauce with 1 tablespoon of water. Set aside.

3  Put the prepared filling ingredients in individual bowls. Get ready a large shallow dish of warm water and a clean, damp tea towel.

4  Submerge a rice paper wrapper in the warm water for 30 seconds (or up to 1 minute) to soften, then remove and place on the tea towel. Smear a little of the yellow bean paste down the middle of the wrapper and top with a little each of the shredded lettuce, noodles, spring onions, cucumber, chilli and pork, and top with a basil leaf. Don't add too much filling or the wrapper will be tricky to roll.

5  Fold the edge of the wrapper closest to you over the filling and tuck in both ends, then roll up tightly to make a neat roll. Set aside on a serving plate and repeat with the remaining wrappers and filling ingredients to make 25 rolls in total. Cover the rolls with the damp tea towel to stop them drying out. Serve with the dipping sauce on the side.

# PANDAN CHICKEN

**You'll find pandan leaves in most Asian grocers, or online. The plant is known as the 'Vanilla of Asia', as it brings a distinct vanilla aroma to Southeast Asian, including Thai, cuisine.**

**SERVES** 4
**PREP** 40 minutes, plus marinating
**COOK** 25 minutes

4 tablespoons light soy sauce
1 tablespoon dark soy sauce
40ml/1¼fl oz coconut milk
4 tablespoons oyster sauce
½ teaspoon salt
a pinch of caster sugar
a pinch of ground white pepper
30g/1oz garlic, chopped
½ teaspoon black peppercorns, cracked
50g/1¾oz coriander stalks, finely chopped
450g/1lb skinless, boneless chicken thighs, cut into 2cm/¾in cubes
about 12 pandan leaves
vegetable oil, for deep-frying

**FOR THE SAUCE**
70g/2½oz caster sugar
2 tablespoons distilled white vinegar
10g/¼oz toasted sesame seeds
2 tablespoons sesame oil
2½ tablespoons dark soy sauce

1  In a large mixing bowl, mix together both types of soy sauce, the coconut milk, oyster sauce, salt, sugar, white pepper, garlic, cracked peppercorns and coriander stalks. Add the chicken pieces, cover and marinate for at least 2 hours, or preferably overnight if time allows, in the fridge, to let the flavours develop.

2  To make the sauce, put 4 tablespoons of water in a small saucepan. Add the sugar and warm over a low heat, stirring occasionally, until dissolved. Add the remaining ingredients and bring to the boil, then reduce the heat to low and simmer for 10 minutes, stirring occasionally, until reduced and thickened. Pour the sauce into a bowl and allow to cool to room temperature.

3  Using a slotted spoon, remove the chicken from the marinade, then discard it.

4  Next, wrap the chicken in the pandan leaves to make 8–12 parcels. To do this, take 3 pieces of the marinated chicken and place them on a leaf, about 7cm/2¾in from the top. Fold the longest part of the leaf over the chicken and continue, until the chicken is completely covered and looks like a triangular-shaped parcel. Tie the ends of the leaf together into a knot, then secure the parcel with a cocktail stick, if you like.

5  Pour enough oil into a large wok (use a wok stand to keep the pan stable), saucepan or deep-fat fryer to deep-fry the parcels. Heat the oil to 180°C/350°F or until a cube of day-old bread turns crisp and golden in 45 seconds.

6  Add the parcels to the hot oil and deep-fry for 4–5 minutes, until the leaves darken slightly around the edges. (You may need to cook them in two batches.) Scoop out the parcels with a slotted spoon and set aside to drain on kitchen paper. Remove the cocktail sticks, if using.

7  Arrange the chicken parcels on a serving plate and serve with the sauce on the side for dipping.

# BANG-KICK PRAWNS

**We put these delicious deep-fried prawns coated in a hot mayo sauce on one of our summer menus, as a special. They were an instant hit.**

**SERVES** 4
**PREP** 20 minutes
**COOK** 5 minutes

100g/3½oz self-raising flour
175g/6oz rice flour
a pinch of salt
vegetable oil, for deep-frying
24 raw king or tiger prawns, peeled, deveined, rinsed and patted dry

**FOR THE HOT MAYO SAUCE**
6 garlic cloves, roughly chopped
2 small Thai red chillies, finely chopped
1 tablespoon Thai shrimp paste
4 tablespoons mayonnaise

**TO SERVE**
1 Little Gem lettuce, finely sliced
1 small ripe mango, peeled, stoned and cut into 1cm/½in dice
1 Thai red chilli, thinly sliced into rings
5 Thai basil leaves or regular basil, finely sliced
1 lime, cut into quarters

1 First, make the sauce. Put the garlic and red chillies in a pestle and mortar, or use a mini food processor or grinder, and grind until smooth. Stir in the shrimp paste and 3 tablespoons of water to make a smooth paste. Spoon the mayonnaise into a medium mixing bowl, then stir in the paste until combined. Set aside.

2 Next, make a batter. Mix together the self-raising flour, 100g/3½oz of the rice flour and the salt in a large mixing bowl. Make a well in the centre and gradually pour in 200ml/7fl oz of water, whisking continuously and drawing the dry ingredients into the wet to make a smooth batter. Set aside.

3 Pour enough oil into a large wok (use a wok stand to keep the pan stable), saucepan or deep-fat fryer to deep-fry the prawns. Heat the oil to 180°C/350°F or until a cube of day-old bread turns crisp and golden in 45 seconds.

4 While the oil is heating, put the remaining rice flour in a medium mixing bowl, toss in the prawns and turn until coated. Place the prawns in a sieve and shake off any excess flour. Next, using tongs, dunk half of the prawns in the batter until coated all over.

5 Place half of the batter-coated prawns in the hot oil and deep-fry for 2 minutes or until crisp and golden brown. Scoop out with a slotted spoon and set aside to drain on kitchen paper. Repeat with the remaining prawns until they are all cooked.

6 When all the prawns have been fried, add them to the bowl with the sauce and turn them until evenly coated.

7 To serve, arrange the lettuce on a serving plate. Pile the prawns on top and scatter over the mango, chilli and basil. Finally, arrange the lime quarters on the side for squeezing over.

# CALAMARI WITH CORIANDER & GINGER PEPPER SAUCE

This is a slight variation on our Busaba menu favourite. Score the calamari once you have cut it into squares as this will help tenderize the flesh and allow it to become nice and crisp during cooking. You'll find fresh green peppercorns in Asian grocers.

**SERVES** 4
**PREP** 20 minutes
**COOK** 20 minutes

4 large cleaned and prepared
    squid tubes
1 egg white, lightly beaten
a pinch of ground white pepper
200g/7oz rice flour
1 sliced lemongrass leaf,
    to garnish

**FOR THE CORIANDER & GINGER
    PEPPER SAUCE**
50ml/1¾fl oz vegetable oil, plus
    extra for deep-frying
5 garlic cloves, finely chopped
20g/¾oz root ginger, peeled and
    finely chopped
1 teaspoon black peppercorns,
    cracked
8 coriander sprigs, stalks and
    leaves separated
5 fresh green peppercorn sprigs,
    peppercorns picked, plus 1 extra
    sprig, cut into 4 small bunches,
    to garnish
2 tablespoons oyster sauce
a pinch of caster sugar

1  Cut the squid into 4cm/1½in squares and, using a very sharp knife, score the flesh into a 5mm/¼in diamond pattern (a craft knife is good for this). Place the squid in a medium mixing bowl, massage in the egg white and white pepper, then cover and refrigerate for 15 minutes.

2  Meanwhile, make the coriander and ginger pepper sauce. Heat a medium wok or frying pan over a medium heat. Pour in the oil and add the garlic, ginger, cracked peppercorns and coriander stalks and stir-fry for 3 minutes. Add the picked green peppercorns, oyster sauce, and sugar. Increase the heat to high, add 4 tablespoons of water and cook, stirring regularly, for 2 minutes, until the peppercorns are tender. Using a hand-held blender, blitz the sauce until smooth, then set aside.

3  Pour enough oil into a large wok (use a wok stand to keep the pan stable), saucepan or deep-fat fryer to deep-fry the calamari. Heat the oil to 180°C/350°F or until a cube of day-old bread turns crisp and golden in 45 seconds.

4  Put the flour in a separate mixing bowl. Remove a quarter of the calamari from the egg white and dunk it in the flour, shaking off any excess.

5  Place the flour-coated calamari in the hot oil and deep-fry for 3 minutes or until crisp and golden. Scoop out with a slotted spoon and drain on kitchen paper. Flour and deep-fry the remaining calamari in batches.

6 To serve, reheat the sauce, then add the calamari, turning them through the sauce until coated. Arrange on a serving platter and garnish with the lemongrass leaf slices, coriander leaves and green peppercorn sprigs.

# THAI STEAMED BUNS

Light and fluffy steamed stuffed buns are a popular snack throughout Southeast Asia. In this version, the Thai-style filling of chicken, ginger and oyster sauce is steamed inside the bun, rather than stuffed into the bun after it's cooked as you would with Vietnamese *bao*. Serve the buns with sweet chilli sauce for dipping.

**MAKES** 12
**PREP** 30 minutes, plus marinating and rising
**COOK** 55 minutes (or less if you have a tiered steamer)

225g/8oz skinless, boneless chicken thighs, finely chopped
2.5cm/1in piece of root ginger, peeled and finely grated
2 garlic cloves, finely grated
1 tablespoon sesame oil
2 tablespoons dark soy sauce
2 tablespoons oyster sauce
85g/3oz white cabbage, finely chopped
4 spring onions, finely chopped
ground white pepper
Sweet Chilli Sauce (see page 257) or sriracha sauce, to serve

**FOR THE DOUGH**
1 tablespoon caster sugar
1 teaspoon dried instant yeast
350g/12oz plain flour, plus extra for dusting
½ teaspoon salt
1½ teaspoons baking powder

1  To make the filling, mix together the chicken, ginger, garlic, 2 teaspoons of the sesame oil, and the soy and oyster sauces, until combined. Season with pepper, cover and leave to marinate in the fridge for at least 2 hours, or preferably overnight.

2  To make the dough, pour 250ml/9fl oz of lukewarm water into a bowl, sprinkle over the sugar and yeast and stir until the sugar dissolves. Set aside for 10 minutes, until frothy on top. Mix together the flour and salt in a large mixing bowl, then make a well in the middle. Pour the yeasted mixture into the well and gradually mix in the flour using a fork, then use your hands to make a ball of dough.

3  Turn the dough out onto a floured surface. Knead for 10 minutes, until smooth and elastic, adding a little more flour if it is too sticky. Wipe the inside of the cleaned mixing bowl with the remaining sesame oil, add the dough and turn to coat it in the oil. Cover the bowl with cling film and leave in a warm place until doubled in size, about 2 hours.

4  Meanwhile, heat a large wok or frying pan over a high heat, add the filling mixture and stir-fry for 6 minutes, until the chicken is cooked and coated in a dark, sticky sauce. Stir in the cabbage and stir-fry for another minute. Transfer to a bowl, stir in the spring onions and leave to cool.

5  Remove the risen dough from the bowl and flatten into an even round. Sprinkle over the baking powder and knead briefly until combined. Divide into 12 balls. Take one ball and flatten it into a round, about 5mm/¼in thick. Put a heaped tablespoon of the chicken mixture in the middle, pull up the edges of the dough around the filling and press together at the top to seal. Set aside on a lightly floured surface. Repeat to make 12 buns.

6  Place each bun on a square of baking paper and then in a bamboo steamer, leaving enough room for them to expand as they cook. (You could use a regular steamer if you don't have a bamboo one.) Cover and steam over a wok of simmering water for 15 minutes, until risen and fluffy. Repeat until you have cooked all the buns. Serve the buns warm with sweet chilli dipping sauce or sriracha sauce.

# ROTI WITH SOFT EGG, AVOCADO & SWEET CHILLI SAUCE

A marriage of cooking styles and influences, this East-meets-West brunch features a flaky roti flatbread topped with a runny poached egg, rocket leaves, ripe avocado, our own sweet chilli sauce, and roasted peanuts and fresh coriander, with a squeeze of zingy lime adding the finishing touch, if you wish. Delicious!

**SERVES** 4
**PREP** 25 minutes, plus resting
**COOK** 25 minutes

300g/10½oz plain flour, plus extra
    for dusting
1 teaspoon baking powder
¾ teaspoon salt
30g/1oz butter or coconut oil,
    melted
4 large eggs

**TO SERVE**
2 large handfuls rocket leaves
2 avocados, cut in half, stone
    and skin removed, and sliced
    lengthways
2 spring onions, thinly sliced
    diagonally
2 tablespoons Sweet Chilli Sauce
    (see page 257) or sriracha sauce
a handful roasted unsalted peanuts,
    roughly chopped
a handful coriander leaves,
    chopped
1 lime, cut into wedges (optional)
salt and freshly ground black
    pepper

1 Mix together the flour, baking powder and salt in a large mixing bowl and make a well in the centre.

2 Pour 230ml/7¾fl oz of lukewarm water into the dry ingredients. Mix with a fork, then with your hands to form a ball of dough, adding a splash more water if needed. Turn the dough out onto a lightly floured work surface and knead for 5 minutes, until smooth. Place the dough in a clean bowl, cover with cling film and leave to rest for 30 minutes.

3 Divide the dough into eight portions and roll each one into a ball. Take one of the balls (keep the others covered with cling film) and roll it out into a thin round, about 18cm/7in in diameter. Brush the top with the melted butter or coconut oil and roll up into a cylinder. Turn the cylinder round so that the short end is facing towards you and roll it up again. Flatten the dough with the palm of your hand and roll it out again into a 18cm/7in round.

4 Heat a large dry wok or frying pan over a high heat, place the roti in the pan and cook for 2 minutes on each side, until flaky and golden. Wrap the roti in foil and keep warm in a low oven while you make the remaining seven roti.

5 Five minutes before you finish cooking the roti, start to poach the eggs. Heat a large pan of water to simmering point, then swirl the water clockwise. Crack one of the eggs into a cup, then gently tip it into the water. Repeat with the remaining eggs. Cook the eggs over a medium–low heat for 3 minutes, until the whites are set but the yolks are runny. Remove the eggs with a slotted spoon and drain briefly on kitchen paper.

6 To serve, put one or two roti on each serving plate and top with the rocket, avocado and spring onions. Arrange a poached egg on top, a spoonful of sweet chilli sauce or sriracha sauce, and a scattering of peanuts and coriander. Season with salt and pepper and finish with a wedge of lime for squeezing over, if using.

# CRAB & CORN FRITTERS WITH SRIRACHA MAYO

**This snack is a seafood variation of a Thai–Chinese vegetarian recipe popular at the October 'Jay' vegetarian festival held annually in Bangkok. Here, we've added crabmeat to give more texture and flavour, but you could leave it out to stick closer to the vegetarian original.**

**SERVES** 4
**PREP** 15 minutes
**COOK** 20 minutes

100g/3½oz self-raising flour
150g/5½oz rice flour
1 teaspoon salt
1 teaspoon ground white pepper
1 teaspoon distilled white vinegar
finely chopped zest of 1 lime
5g/⅛oz Thai basil leaves or regular
    basil, finely chopped
150g/5½oz cooked sweetcorn,
    cooked fresh or frozen, or
    canned (drained weight)
150g/5½oz white crabmeat
vegetable oil, for deep-frying
1 lime, cut into quarters, to serve

**FOR THE SRIRACHA MAYO**
40g/1½oz sriracha sauce
40g/1½oz mayonnaise

1  Make the sriracha mayo by mixing together the ingredients in a small bowl to combine. Set aside.

2  To make the fritters, mix together the both types of flour in a large mixing bowl. Gradually, whisk in 200ml/7fl oz of water to make a smooth batter. Stir in the salt, pepper, vinegar, lime zest and basil until thoroughly combined. Leave the batter to rest for 20–30 minutes so that it doesn't become too dense during cooking.

3  After resting, fold in the sweetcorn and crabmeat, taking care not to break up the crab too much. Set aside briefly while you heat the oil.

4  Pour enough oil into a large wok (use a wok stand to keep the pan stable), saucepan or deep-fat fryer to deep-fry the fritters. Heat the oil to 180°C/350°F or until a cube of day-old bread turns crisp and golden in 45 seconds.

5  Using a dessert spoon, carefully place a spoonful of the crab mixture into the hot oil. Repeat to cook about 4 fritters at a time, depending on the size of your pan. Deep-fry the fritters for 3 minutes, then turn them over using a slotted spoon or chopstick and cook for another 3 minutes or until crisp and golden brown. Scoop out the fritters with a slotted spoon and drain on kitchen paper. Repeat to make 8–12 fritters in total, keeping the cooked fritters warm in a low oven. Serve the fritters with the sriracha mayo and lime wedges.

The 'Tesagan Gin Jay' (shortened simply to 'Jay') vegetarian festival is a buzz of street food, drumbeats and processions held every year in the Chinatown district of Bangkok. It occurs during the ninth lunar month of the Chinese calendar, which usually falls in October.

# PORK & PRAWN WONTON

You can find different versions of dumplings, or wonton, all over Southeast Asia and these steamed ones come with a classic pork, prawn and oyster sauce filling and chilli-soy dipping sauce. A goji berry adds a splash of colour to the top of the open dumpling, but isn't essential. Make sure you use wonton wrappers for steaming, rather than deep-frying – you'll find them in Asian grocers in the chilled or freezer cabinet.

**MAKES** 16
**PREP** 25 minutes
**COOK** 10–20 minutes

100g/3½oz pork mince
100g/3½oz raw peeled tiger prawns, deveined and very finely chopped
2 spring onions, finely chopped
2 garlic cloves, finely grated
4cm/1½in piece of root ginger, peeled and finely grated
1 teaspoon sesame oil
2 tablespoons oyster sauce
16 wonton wrappers for steaming, defrosted if frozen
16 dried goji berries (optional)
salt and ground white pepper

**FOR THE DIPPING SAUCE**
2 tablespoons Sweet Chilli Sauce (see page 257) or sriracha sauce
1 tablespoon light soy sauce
2 teaspoons fish sauce
1 tablespoon lime juice
¼–½ teaspoon dried chilli flakes, to taste

1  Mix together all the ingredients for the dipping sauce with 1 tablespoon of warm water and set aside.

2  Mix together the pork, prawns, spring onions, garlic, ginger, sesame oil and oyster sauce in a large mixing bowl. Season with salt and pepper.

3  To make the wonton, place a heaped tablespoon of the pork mixture in the middle of a wonton wrapper (keep the others covered with a damp tea towel to stop them drying out). Brush the edges with a little water, then gather the wonton up around the filling, tap the bottom to flatten it slightly and leave the top open. Place a goji berry, if using, on top of the open dumpling. Cover with a damp cloth and repeat with the remaining wrappers and filling to make 16 dumplings in total.

4  Place each wonton on a small square of baking paper and then in a large bamboo steamer or regular steamer. (Use a double-tiered steamer if you have one; if not you may need to cook the wonton in two batches.) Cover and steam over a wok or pan of simmering water for 8–10 minutes, adding extra water if needed. Serve the wonton straightaway with the dipping sauce.

# THAI FISHCAKES

**You'll find Thai fishcakes in every street-food market in Bangkok and throughout Thailand. This recipe combines white fish and prawns with Thai red curry paste and aromatics to create a slightly spicy and salty cake. Cucumber relish and chilli tomato sauce balance the flavours.**

**SERVES** 4
**PREP** 20 minutes, plus chilling
**COOK** 20 minutes

400g/14oz skinless thick white fish fillets, such as cod, haddock or pollack, pin-boned
200g/7oz raw peeled king or tiger prawns, deveined and roughly chopped
80g/2¾oz Red Curry Paste (see page 254) or ready-made paste
2 tablespoons fish sauce
a pinch of caster sugar
10 fresh kaffir lime leaves, finely shredded
10g/¼oz Thai basil leaves or regular basil, finely chopped
40g/1½oz snake beans or fine French beans, very thinly sliced
10g/¼oz krachai (wild ginger), finely chopped (optional)
vegetable oil, for greasing and deep-frying
½ recipe quantity Sweet Chilli Tomato Sauce (see page 257) or sriracha sauce, to serve
1 lime, cut into wedges, to serve

**FOR THE CUCUMBER & PEANUT RELISH**
½ cucumber, deseeded and thinly sliced
1 banana shallot, thinly sliced
1 large red chilli, deseeded and chopped
1 tablespoon roasted unsalted peanuts, finely chopped

1  Put the fish and prawns in a food processor and blend to a smooth paste. Spoon the mixture into a large mixing bowl and add the red curry paste, fish sauce, sugar, kaffir lime leaves, basil, beans, and krachai, if using.

2  Lightly grease your hands with a little vegetable oil (or, use disposable gloves) and knead the fish mixture until all the ingredients are thoroughly combined into a smooth paste. Cover and refrigerate for 2 hours to allow the mixture to firm up.

3  When ready, roll the fish mixture into 12 x 3cm/1¼in balls. Place the balls on a lightly oiled tray and gently press each one down to form a patty, about 5mm/¼in thick. Cover and refrigerate for about 30 minutes to firm up.

4  Meanwhile, make the cucumber and peanut relish. Put the cucumber, shallot and chilli in a serving bowl and mix in 1 tablespoon of the sweet chilli tomato sauce. Sprinkle the peanuts over the top. Set aside.

5  Pour enough oil into a large wok (use a wok stand to keep the pan stable), saucepan or deep-fat fryer to deep-fry the fishcakes. Heat the oil to 180°C/350°F or until a cube of day-old bread turns crisp and golden in 45 seconds.

6  Place 4 of the fishcakes into the hot oil and deep-fry for 2–3 minutes, then turn them over using a slotted spoon or chopstick and cook for another 2–3 minutes, until crisp and golden brown. Scoop out the fishcakes with a slotted spoon and drain on kitchen paper. Repeat twice more to make 12 fishcakes in total, keeping the cooked fishcakes warm in a low oven.

7  Spoon the remaining sweet chilli tomato sauce over the cucumber relish. Arrange the fritters on a serving plate and serve with the cucumber relish for scooping, and wedges of lime.

# RICE PANCAKE WRAPS

The secret to the success of these turmeric-coloured pancakes is to get all the filling ingredients prepared and ready to go before you start cooking. Organization is key: the pancake stays warm without overcooking while you add a mixture of smoked tofu, peanuts, vegetables, chilli and herbs. For a meat or seafood alternative to tofu, add strips of roasted pork or chicken, wok-fried prawns or strips of golden fried fish.

**MAKES** 8
**PREP** 20 minutes, plus resting
**COOK** 20 minutes

100g/3½oz rice flour
60g/2¼oz plain flour
½ teaspoon ground turmeric
½ teaspoon salt
200ml/7fl oz coconut milk
2 eggs, lightly beaten
groundnut oil, for frying
ground white pepper

**FOR THE FILLING**
300g/10½oz smoked tofu, cut into
    long strips, about 1cm/½in wide
5 spring onions, cut into long strips
1 red pepper, deseeded and cut into
    thin strips
2 handfuls beansprouts
2 handfuls coriander leaves
55g/2oz roasted unsalted peanuts,
    roughly chopped
3 tablespoons Sweet Chilli Sauce
    (see page 257) or sriracha sauce

1  First, make the rice pancakes. Mix together both types of flour, the turmeric and salt in a large mixing bowl, then make a well in the centre. Whisk together the coconut milk, eggs and 70ml/2¼fl oz of water. Gradually, pour the egg mixture into the flour mixture, whisking to make a smooth batter. Season with pepper and leave to rest for at least 15 minutes at room temperature.

2  While the batter is resting, organize the filling ingredients into individual bowls.

3  Heat a medium wok or frying pan over a medium heat. Add a splash of oil and swirl it around the base. Add 55ml/1¾fl oz of the batter and quickly swirl the wok or pan to spread the batter into a thin pancake. Cook for 1–2 minutes or until the base of the pancake starts to colour and the top is almost cooked. Place a few slices of tofu, spring onion, red pepper, beansprouts, coriander, peanuts and a drizzle of chilli or sriracha sauce in the middle, fold the pancake over the filling and slip it onto a serving plate.

4  Serve the wrap straightaway or keep it warm, covered, in a low oven while you make a further 7 wraps.

# CRAB STUFFED OMELETTE

**Super-satisfying and easy to make, stuffed omelette is popular street-food fare in Bangkok. This one is filled with crab, but you could try strips of cooked pork or chicken, prawns, crispy tofu or steamed or stir-fried vegetables (mushrooms are particularly delicious) instead.**

**SERVES** 4
**PREP** 10 minutes
**COOK** 15 minutes

4 teaspoons groundnut oil
8 eggs
2 teaspoons light soy sauce
125g/4½oz white crabmeat
2 spring onions, thinly sliced
    diagonally
1 medium-hot red chilli, deseeded
    and thinly sliced
a generous handful beansprouts
a handful coriander leaves,
    chopped
juice of ½ lime
ground white pepper
oyster sauce, to serve (optional)
lime wedges, to serve

1  Heat 1 teaspoon of the groundnut oil in large wok or frying pan over a medium heat.

2  Meanwhile, beat 2 of the eggs with ½ teaspoon of the soy sauce and season with pepper. Pour the egg mixture into the wok or pan, swirling the pan so the mixture evenly covers the base. Reduce the heat slightly and cook the omelette for a minute or so until the egg is only slightly runny on top.

3  Spoon a quarter of the crabmeat, spring onions, chilli, beansprouts and coriander into the middle of the omelette. Drizzle over a little of the lime juice, then fold in each side to make a square omelette with the filling inside. Cook briefly in the wok or pan to warm the filling.

4  Slip the omelette onto a plate and serve with a drizzle of oyster sauce, if you like, and wedges of lime on the side. Repeat with the remaining eggs and filling ingredients to make 4 omelettes in total.

In Thailand, crab dishes are mainly the speciality of the southern provinces, where shellfish thrive. White crabmeat comes from the claws of the crab. It has a delicate flavour and is lighter in texture than the rich brown meat found beneath the upper crab shell.

# SOUP

In Thailand, soup is traditionally served as an integral part of a whole meal, rather than a separate course or meal in its own right. Most commonly, a soup is put on the table at the beginning of the meal and remains there until the end to provide light liquid refreshment that counterbalances richer, heavier dishes.

Restorative, healthy and low in fat, soups such as the ubiquitous *tom yam goong* (see page 80) are classically hot and sour, with fresh herbs and spices adding fragrant notes. Every restaurant and every home in Thailand – if not throughout Southeast Asia – will offer it up in slightly different variations. Most often, though, it is delicate and light and infused with lemongrass, kaffir lime leaves, coriander, chilli, lime juice and fish sauce. The result is a broth that is balanced in flavour and enchantingly aromatic. Thai cooks then add to this base – chicken, pork, vegetables, noodles, fish, shellfish and tofu are all options, depending on how substantial the soup is to be.

In Thai cooking, the stock is the essence of the soup. Whether it's a clear broth, or something creamy, rich and coconutty, the stock is where it all begins. As a basic rule of thumb, make it match: so chicken stock for chicken soup, fish stock for fish soup and so on. All that said, water rather than stock is sometimes enough. For example, in the Beef Brisket Noodle Soup (see page 81) the brisket is cooked in water first to make the base of the broth without the need for additional stock.

The lighter broth-based soups in this chapter are all perfect for serving the Thai way – for guests to help themselves throughout a meal. But, in the spirit of Thai-fusion cooking, we've also included some more substantial soups that need little in the way of accompaniment and make a filling lunch or dinner in themselves. Try, for example, the laksa-style soup on page 86. Although Malaysian in origin, laksa appears in all sorts of guises throughout Thailand, too. And, as far as we're concerned, the addition of coconut milk makes it all the more luxurious.

When serving soups, offer your guests extra flavourings and seasonings to sprinkle onto their soup just before eating. A sprinkling of fresh herbs, fresh or dried chillies or fried slivers of garlic will boost flavour, colour and texture, while a dash of soy sauce, chilli sauce or sriracha sauce will give a flavour hit that lifts a soup to another level.

# PORK BALLS IN FRAGRANT THAI BROTH

This light broth is packed with flavour and contains rice noodles to make it more substantial. You could leave out the noodles if you wanted to serve it in the traditional Thai way: placed on the dining table at the start of the meal and left there throughout so that you and your guests can eat it as and when you need something to hydrate you.

**SERVES** 4
**PREP** 20 minutes
**COOK** 30 minutes

400g/14oz pork mince
1 banana shallot, finely chopped
3 tablespoons chopped coriander leaves
4cm/1½in piece of root ginger, peeled and finely grated
2 garlic cloves, finely grated
2 tablespoons fish sauce
2 tablespoons cornflour
1 medium-hot red chilli, deseeded and diced
225g/8oz rice ribbon noodles
4 pak choi, cut in half or quarters, if large
a large handful beansprouts
salt and ground white pepper

**FOR THE BROTH**
1 tablespoon rapeseed oil
4 spring onions, white and green parts separated, thinly sliced diagonally
1 litre/35fl oz chicken stock
4cm/1½in piece of root ginger, peeled and cut into 3mm/⅛in thick slices
1 Thai red chilli, split in half, deseeded if preferred, plus extra thinly sliced, to serve (optional)
2 lemongrass sticks, bruised
a handful coriander stalks, chopped, plus extra leaves to garnish
4 kaffir lime leaves
1 tablespoon fish sauce

1  To make the pork balls, break up the mince in a large mixing bowl with a fork, then stir in the remaining ingredients up to and including the chilli, until combined. Season with salt and pepper. With damp hands, form the pork mixture into 20 walnut-sized balls and set aside, covered, in the fridge until needed.

2  To make the broth, heat the oil in a large wok or saucepan over a high heat and stir-fry the white part of the spring onions for 2 minutes, then add the stock, ginger, chilli, lemongrass, coriander stalks, lime leaves and fish sauce. Bring to the boil, then reduce the heat and simmer, part-covered with a lid, for 15 minutes so that the flavours infuse the broth.

3  Meanwhile, cook the noodles following the instructions on the packet, then drain and refresh under cold running water. Return the noodles to the pan, cover with cold water and set aside.

4  Add the pork balls to the broth, return to a gentle boil and cook for 7 minutes, then add the pak choi and simmer for another 3 minutes, until tender and the pork balls are cooked through.

5  To serve, drain the noodles and divide them between four large, warmed shallow serving bowls. Ladle the broth, pork balls and pak choi into the bowls, topping each serving with extra coriander leaves, the green part of the spring onions, a mound of beansprouts, and extra chilli, if you like.

# MIXED MUSHROOM & GALANGAL NOODLE BOWL

A comforting bowl of steaming broth, this filling vegetarian dish is made with three different types of mushroom – intensely flavoured dried shiitake, frilly-looking wood ear and earthy chestnut. You can find dried mushrooms in most Asian grocers and they will keep for months stored in an airtight container – wood ears are very light so a little weight goes a long way.

**SERVES** 4
**PREP** 15 minutes, plus soaking
**COOK** 25 minutes

40g/1½oz dried shiitake
    mushrooms
5g/⅛oz dried wood ear mushrooms
    (black fungus)
200g/7oz rice ribbon noodles
1 tablespoon groundnut oil
175g/6oz chestnut mushrooms,
    sliced
2 garlic cloves, thinly sliced
1 Thai red chilli, split lengthways
    and deseeded
5cm/2in piece of galangal, peeled
    and sliced into thin 5mm/¼in
    thick rounds
850ml/29fl oz hot vegetable stock
2 tablespoons dark soy sauce
100g/3½oz spring greens or
    cabbage, shredded
100g/3½oz silken tofu, drained well
    and cut into bite-sized cubes
a handful coriander leaves, to serve

1  Put the dried shiitake and wood ear mushrooms in separate heatproof bowls. Pour 200ml/7fl oz of just-boiled water from a kettle over the shiitake. Pour enough hot water over the wood ear mushrooms to cover. Leave the mushrooms to soften for 20 minutes.

2  Meanwhile, cook the noodles following the instructions on the packet, then drain and refresh under cold running water. Return the noodles to the pan, cover with cold water and set aside.

3  When the dried mushrooms are ready, drain the shiitake, reserving the soaking water. Drain the wood ear, discarding their soaking water. Slice the shiitake, discarding any tough stalks, and roughly tear the wood ear into large bite-sized pieces.

4  Heat a large wok or saucepan over a high heat. Add the oil and when hot add the chestnut mushrooms and rehydrated shiitake and stir-fry for 6 minutes, until softened. Add the garlic, chilli, galangal and wood ears and stir-fry for another minute.

5  Pour in the stock, shiitake soaking water and soy sauce. Bring to the boil, then reduce the heat to medium–low and simmer, part-covered with a lid, for 10 minutes. Add the spring greens or cabbage and cook for 3 minutes, until just tender.

6  Drain the noodles and divide them between four warmed large shallow serving bowls. Add equal amounts of tofu to each bowl, then ladle over equal amounts of the hot vegetable broth, picking out the chilli as you go (you can also remove the galangal if you wish, although traditionally it's left in and eaten). Sprinkle with coriander before serving.

# TOM YAM GOONG

Arguably Thailand's most famous soup, *tom yam goong* originated from central Thailand and is known all over the world. A clear, light and spicy prawn soup, full of Thai flavour and aroma, it is usually finished with freshly picked garden herbs.

**SERVES** 4
**PREP** 15 minutes
**COOK** 10 minutes

1.5 litres/52fl oz vegetable stock
2 lemongrass stalks, bruised and
  cut into 2.5cm/1in lengths
80g/2¾oz piece of galangal,
  thinly sliced
8 kaffir lime leaves, torn
50g/1¾oz coriander sprigs, stalks
  and leaves separated
4 tablespoons fish sauce
8 raw peeled king or tiger prawns,
  deveined
200g/7oz oyster mushrooms,
  trimmed and cut in half
4 Thai red chillies, bruised
1 tomato, deseeded and cut
  into small dice
juice of 1 lime

**1** Pour the vegetable stock into a large saucepan, add the lemongrass, galangal, kaffir lime leaves, coriander stalks and fish sauce, then bring to the boil. Reduce the heat to medium and simmer for 3 minutes.

**2** Reduce the heat to low, add the prawns and mushrooms and simmer for 4 minutes or until the prawns are cooked through.

**3** Just before serving, add the chillies, tomato dice and lime juice. Then, ladle the soup into four warmed large serving bowls, sprinkle over the coriander leaves and bring to the table.

# BEEF BRISKET NOODLE SOUP

A lunchtime Thai favourite, this noodle-based soup pops up throughout Bangkok in the city's vibrant cafés. Make it personal by serving sriracha sauce, light soy sauce and fish sauce alongside to suit your taste buds.

**SERVES** 4–6
**PREP** 20 minutes
**COOK** 4 hours

1kg/2lb 4oz beef brisket, trimmed and cut into 2.5cm/1in cubes
1 teaspoon ground white pepper
1 cinnamon stick
10 garlic cloves, bruised
50g/1¾oz coriander sprigs, stalks and leaves separated, chopped
200ml/7fl oz light soy sauce
5 tablespoons oyster sauce
5 tablespoons soy bean paste
5 heads Chinese broccoli (gai lan or kailan), cut into 4cm/1½in pieces
400g/14oz beansprouts
200g/7oz rice vermicelli noodles
1 thinly sliced spring onion and 1 thinly sliced Thai red chilli, to garnish
sriracha sauce, light soy sauce and fish sauce, to serve (optional)

1  Season the beef with the pepper, rubbing in the pepper all over.

2  Pour 3 litres/105fl oz of water into a large saucepan, add the cinnamon stick, garlic, coriander stalks, soy sauce, oyster sauce and soy bean paste and bring to the boil.

3  When the liquid is boiling, add the beef brisket, then reduce the heat to low. Cover with a lid and cook for 3 hours, until the liquid reduces by about half. Pour in another 3 litres/105fl oz of water and continue to cook for another 1 hour, covered, or until the brisket is very tender.

4  Meanwhile, bring a medium pan of water to the boil and cook the Chinese broccoli and beansprouts for 2 minutes, until the broccoli is just tender. Drain and refresh under cold running water.

5  Soak the rice noodles in hot water for 2–3 minutes, until tender. Drain the noodles and divide them equally between four warmed large serving bowls along with the Chinese broccoli and beansprouts.

6  Strain the broth and remove the cinnamon stick. Divide the beef and coriander stalks equally between the serving bowls and ladle over the broth. (You will probably have some broth left over – leave it to cool, then transfer it to a freezer-proof container and freeze it to use another time.)

7  Just before serving, sprinkle over the coriander leaves, spring onion and chilli, then provide sriracha sauce, light soy sauce and fish sauce at the table to let everyone help themselves and flavour the soup to their taste.

# TOM KLONG CHICKEN NOODLE SOUP

This is a *tom-yam*-style soup from rural Thailand. Traditionally, the ingredients would be smoked before cooking, and the pieces of galangal and lemongrass are left in to be chewed or sucked!

**SERVES** 4
**PREP** 15 minutes
**COOK** 15 minutes

4 whole dried chillies (optional)
1.5 litres/52fl oz chicken stock
2 lemongrass stalks, peeled and
    thinly sliced diagonally
50g/1¾oz coriander sprigs, stalks
    and leaves separated
6 kaffir lime leaves
30g/1oz piece of galangal, cut into
    5mm/¼in thick slices
125ml/4fl oz fish sauce
4 banana shallots, thinly cut into
    rings
2 boneless, skinless chicken
    breasts, cut into strips diagonally
    (about 8 slices per breast)
100g/3½oz oyster mushrooms,
    trimmed and cut in half
100g/3½oz shimeji mushrooms,
    trimmed
juice of 1 lime
4 Thai red chillies, bruised
a handful coriander and basil
    leaves

**1** First, toast the dried chillies, if using. Preheat the grill to medium and grill the chillies for 2–3 minutes, turning once, until they smell aromatic. Remove from the heat and leave to cool.

**2** Pour the chicken stock into a large saucepan and bring to the boil. Add the lemongrass, coriander stalks, kaffir lime leaves, galangal, fish sauce, shallots and chicken, then reduce the heat to medium and simmer for 5 minutes. Add both types of mushroom and simmer for a further 5 minutes, then stir in the lime juice and warm through.

**3** Ladle the soup into four warmed large serving bowls and top each bowl with a bruised red chilli and a sprinkling of coriander and basil leaves, then crumble the toasted dried chillies over the top to serve, if using. Traditionally, you would eat all the ingredients in the soup, but feel free to leave the lemongrass and galangal, if you prefer.

# KANOM JIN CHICKEN LAKSA

A laksa is a lightly spicy noodle soup, here made with thin rice noodles, known as *kanom jin*. The soup is popular in all of the Thai culinary regions, each with its own local variation. The key ingredients that are always there are the coconut milk, krachai (wild ginger) and chilli.

**SERVES** 4
**PREP** 20 minutes
**COOK** 45 minutes

200g/7oz kanom jin or somen noodles (note that somen noodles are not gluten-free)
4 boneless, skinless chicken breasts, about 175g/6oz each
165g/5¾oz beansprouts, plus extra for serving

**FOR THE LAKSA SAUCE**
70ml/2¼fl oz vegetable oil
8 garlic cloves, finely chopped
100g/3½oz krachai (wild ginger), finely chopped
8 banana shallots, finely chopped
200g/7oz Red Curry Paste (see page 254) or ready-made paste
2 tablespoons palm sugar or light soft brown sugar
800ml/28fl oz coconut milk
8 kaffir lime leaves, torn in half
125ml/4fl oz fish sauce

**TO SERVE**
50g/1¾oz fine green beans, very finely sliced
a handful mint leaves
a handful coriander leaves
1 spring onion, thinly sliced
4 whole dried chillies, toasted (see page 83)

1  First, make the sauce. Heat a medium saucepan over a high heat. Add the oil and fry the garlic, krachai and shallots for 3 minutes, until softened. Add the red curry paste, reduce the heat to medium and cook, stirring, for 3 minutes. Stir in the sugar and cook for 1 minute more.

2  Add the coconut milk, torn kaffir lime leaves, fish sauce and 1.2 litres/40fl oz of water. Bring the soup to the boil, then reduce the heat to medium–low and simmer for a few moments at just below boiling point, then remove the pan from the heat and allow to cool.

3  Meanwhile, cook the noodles following the pack instructions, then drain and plunge into cold water and set aside.

4  In a medium saucepan, bring 2 litres/70fl oz of water to the boil. Add the chicken breasts, cover with a lid and cook over a medium heat for 25 minutes or until cooked through. Remove the chicken from the pan (reserve the cooking liquid to make chicken stock). Cut the cooked chicken breasts into 1cm/½in cubes, then set aside until needed.

5  Just before serving, add the cooked chicken to the laksa sauce and reheat thoroughly.

6  Meanwhile, reheat the cooked noodles in boiling water for 1 minute. Drain and divide them equally between four warmed large serving bowls. Pile equal amounts of the beansprouts on top of each portion. Using a slotted spoon, remove the chicken from the sauce and divide it equally between the bowls, then ladle the sauce over the top.

7  Serve the laksa topped with equal amounts of the green beans, mint, coriander, beansprouts and spring onion, and with the dried chillies crumbled over the top.

# WOK NOODLE

When we ask our customers to name a favourite dish on our menu, pad Thai definitely vies for pole position with red or green curry. This world-famous stir-fried noodle dish is equally as popular in Thailand, where it could even be called the country's national dish. Large, steaming woks of pad Thai are a familiar sight in most street-food markets, mobile food stalls and casual restaurants.

There is no single go-to recipe for pad Thai, yet, whether it features seafood, poultry or meat, or is vegetarian (and just to go against the grain we have a no-noodle pad Thai on page 97, too), the key to the success of the dish is a contrast of textures and a balance of flavours – salty, sour and sweet. Texture comes from the melange of crisp vegetables and beansprouts and crunchy nuts, all offset (most of the time!) by soft, silky noodles.

What all stir-fried noodle dishes, pad Thai included, have in common is that they are quick, easy, tasty and a complete meal in one pan, which goes some way to explain why they've become one of Thailand's top fast foods. When making stir-fried noodles at home, it's so much easier to have all the ingredients prepared and ready to go before you start cooking. Cut any solid ingredients into bite-sized pieces, measure out your liquids and pre-cook or soak your noodles before you even lift the wok. The noodles should also be cold before you toss them as this helps them to keep their shape and prevents them sticking to the base of the pan.

A useful tip is to warm the wok over the hob before you add the oil. This means the oil heats quickly and evenly and you can swirl it like a pro to coat the inside of the pan before adding the rest of the ingredients. A coated wok helps the ingredients to stop catching and sticking. Add your flavourings, such as garlic and ginger next, but they'll need stir-frying only briefly – any longer and you risk that they'll burn and turn bitter. Then, add the ingredients that take the longest to cook. Keep the food moving, tossing and flipping with a wok stirrer or spatula so the contents cook evenly. If the food starts to catch or burn, turn down the heat slightly, or you can add a splash of water or other liquid – but be cautious as you don't want your stir-fry to stew or become watery.

# CLASSIC PAD THAI

During World War II a rice shortage in Thailand led to this now most famous Thai dish – made with stir-fried rice noodles. A well-balanced combination of salty, sour and sweet, *pad Thai* is now an inherent part of Thai culinary identity. For home-cooking ease, this recipe cooks for four people in one go, but the best results – perfect noodles and perfect beansprouts – occur if you can cook each portion individually.

**SERVES** 4
**PREP** 15 minutes
**COOK** 15 minutes

100g/3½oz ribbon rice noodles
3 tablespoons vegetable oil
3 garlic cloves, roughly chopped
1 banana shallot, roughly chopped
16 raw peeled king or tiger prawns, deveined
2 eggs
2 tablespoons finely sliced turnip
1 tablespoon dried shrimp
100ml/3½fl oz Pad Thai Sauce (see page 256)
200g/7oz beansprouts
5 Chinese chives or regular chives, cut into 4cm/1½in lengths
4 tablespoons finely chopped roasted unsalted peanuts, to serve
1 lime, cut into quarters, to serve

1 First, cook the noodles following the instructions on the packet, then drain and refresh under cold running water. Return the noodles to the pan, cover with cold water and set aside.

2 While the noodles are cooking, heat a large wok or frying pan over a medium heat. Add the oil and, when hot, add the garlic and shallot and stir-fry for 1 minute. Next, add the prawns, increase the heat to high and stir-fry for 2 minutes.

3 Crack the eggs into a cup, then tip them into the wok with the turnip and dried shrimp and cook for 2 minutes, stirring continuously, until the eggs are firm and the prawns are cooked.

4 Using a wok ladle or a spatula, move the mixture to one side. Drain the noodles and add them to the empty part of the wok or pan and cook for 2–3 minutes, until heated through. Keep tossing the noodles to stop them sticking to the bottom.

5 When the noodles are hot, toss them together with the prawn and egg mixture, then make a space in the middle for the pad Thai sauce. Pour in the sauce and let it cook for a few minutes until caramelized, then toss in the noodle mixture until combined and cook for another 2 minutes.

6 Add the beansprouts and cook for a further 1 minute. Then, add the chives, stirring gently to prevent the noodles breaking up, and remove from the heat. Transfer the pad Thai to a serving plate, or to individual dishes, and scatter over the peanuts. Serve with wedges of lime on the side.

# PAD THAI JAY

This is the vegetarian cousin of the traditional prawn *pad Thai*. The prawns may be gone, but this recipe still has all the balanced flavours you'd expect, and the tofu makes it nicely substantial.

**SERVES** 4
**PREP** 20 minutes
**COOK** 15 minutes

100g/3½oz ribbon rice noodles
2 tablespoons vegetable oil
1 garlic clove, finely chopped
1 small banana shallot, finely
    chopped
50g/1¾oz fine green beans,
    cut in half
90g/3¼oz Tenderstem broccoli,
    cut in half
1 courgette, cut in half lengthways
    and thinly sliced
60g/2¼oz fried tofu pieces
1 small turnip, finely chopped
100ml/3½fl oz Pad Thai Sauce
    (see page 256)
200g/7oz beansprouts
30g/1oz Chinese chives or regular
    chives, cut into 4cm/1½in
    lengths
4 tablespoons finely chopped
    roasted unsalted peanuts,
    to serve
1 lime, cut into quarters, to serve

1  First, cook the noodles following the instructions on the packet, then drain and refresh under cold running water. Return the noodles to the pan, cover with cold water and set aside.

2  While the noodles are cooking, heat a large wok or frying pan over a medium heat. Add the oil and when hot, add the garlic and shallot and stir-fry for 1 minute. Next, add the green beans, broccoli, courgette, tofu and turnip, then increase the heat to high and stir-fry for 2 minutes, until the vegetables have softened slightly.

3  Using a wok ladle or a spatula, move the mixture to one side. Drain the noodles and add them to the empty part of the wok or pan and cook for 2–3 minutes, until heated through. Keep tossing the noodles to stop them sticking to the bottom.

4  When the noodles are hot, toss them with the vegetable mixture, then make a space in the middle for the pad Thai sauce. Pour in the sauce and let it cook for a few minutes until caramelized, then toss in the noodle mixture until combined and cook for another 2 minutes.

5  Add the beansprouts and cook for a further 1 minute. Then, add the chives, stirring gently to prevent the noodles breaking up, then remove from the heat. Transfer to a serving plate, or to individual dishes, and scatter over the peanuts. Serve with wedges of lime on the side.

# NO-NOODLE PAD THAI

**Some Thais love to eat noodle dishes that do not have noodles! This is a fun and easy recipe to cook. It's incredibly tasty and light and is delicious on its own, or as a side dish for something meaty.**

**SERVES** 4 (as a main)
**PREP** 15 minutes
**COOK** 5 minutes

400g/14oz beansprouts
5 Chinese chives or regular chives, cut into 4cm/1½in lengths
2 tablespoons preserved turnip, finely sliced
1 tablespoon dried shrimp
55g/2oz fried tofu pieces
4 tablespoons roasted unsalted crushed peanuts
5 garlic cloves, roughly chopped
1 banana shallot, thinly sliced
2 tablespoons vegetable oil
1 tablespoon fish sauce
4 teaspoons caster sugar
1 teaspoon chilli powder
2 limes

1  The traditional way to make this is to, first, take a large serving plate and layer the ingredients in the following order: beansprouts, chives, preserved turnip, dried shrimp, fried tofu, peanuts, garlic and finally the shallot on top. Set aside.

2  Heat a large wok or frying pan over a medium heat. Add the oil and when very hot (about 2 minutes), add everything on the plate, flipping the plate over so the garlic and shallots hit the wok or pan first. Alternatively, prepare all the ingredients and add them to the pan in reverse order and stir until mixed together.

3  Add the fish sauce, sugar, chilli powder and the juice of 1 lime, then, using a wok spatula, flip everything for 3 minutes, ensuring the beansprouts are well cooked.

4  Transfer to a serving platter and serve straightaway, with the remaining lime cut into wedges and arranged alongside.

You can easily turn this into a vegan *pad Thai* – just leave out the dried shrimp and replace the fish sauce with the same quantity of soy sauce.

# SMOKED CHICKEN NOODLES

This is a simple stir-fried noodle recipe with only a little richness and smokiness in the dish itself, enabling you to season to taste at the table with sriracha sauce, light soy sauce and chilli flakes.

**SERVES** 4
**PREP** 10 minutes
**COOK** 15 minutes

280g/10oz rice vermicelli noodles
1 tablespoon vegetable oil
4 garlic cloves, finely chopped
4 eggs
1 tablespoon dark soy sauce
140g/5oz Chinese broccoli (gai lan
    or kailan) or long-stem broccoli,
    thinly sliced
100g/3½oz cooked smoked chicken,
    flaked into strips
1 tablespoon fish sauce
a pinch of caster sugar
sriracha sauce, light soy sauce
    and chilli flakes, to serve

1  Put the noodles in a heatproof bowl and pour over enough just-boiled water from a kettle to cover and stir well to loosen. Leave the noodles for 3–5 minutes, until softened, then drain, refresh under cold running water and place in a bowl.

2  Heat a large wok or frying pan over a medium heat. Add the oil and when hot, add the garlic and stir-fry for 1 minute. Crack the eggs into a cup, then tip them into the wok or pan and cook for 2 minutes, stirring continuously, until firm.

3  Increase the heat to high, add the noodles, dark soy sauce, broccoli and smoked chicken and cook for 2 minutes, gently tossing to stop the noodles sticking to the bottom of the wok or pan.

4  Add the fish sauce and sugar and toss gently and continuously for another 2 minutes, until golden and heated through. Remove from the heat and allow to rest for 1 minute before serving with the sriracha sauce, light soy sauce and chilli flakes alongside to allow everyone to season according to their own taste.

# PORK NOODLE LARB

**Fresh herbs, roasted peanuts, ginger, garlic and lime add plenty of flavour, crunch and zing to this classic meat-based salad. Here, the favourite street-food dish is turned into a more substantial meal with the addition of ribbon rice noodles. But, if you want to go down the more traditional route, leave out the noodles and simply serve on top of a bed of crisp salad leaves.**

**SERVES** 4
**PREP** 15 minutes
**COOK** 15 minutes

225g/8oz ribbon rice noodles
2 tablespoons jasmine rice
2 tablespoons rapeseed oil
3 banana shallots, thinly sliced
4 spring onions, white and
    green parts separated, sliced
    diagonally
2 lemongrass sticks, peeled and
    finely chopped
2.5cm/1in piece of root ginger,
    peeled and finely chopped
3 large garlic cloves, finely chopped
1 Thai red chilli, deseeded and
    thinly sliced
500g/1lb 2oz pork mince
2 tablespoons fish sauce
juice of 1 lime, plus extra wedges
    to serve
1 teaspoon palm sugar or light soft
    brown sugar
a large handful coriander leaves,
    chopped
a large handful mint leaves
    chopped
1 Little Gem lettuce, leaves
    separated, to serve
50g/1¾oz roasted unsalted
    peanuts, roughly chopped,
    to serve
salt and ground white pepper

1 First, cook the noodles following the instructions on the packet, then drain and refresh under cold running water. Return the noodles to the pan, cover with cold water and set aside.

2 While the noodles are cooking, heat a large dry wok or frying pan over a medium heat. When hot, add the rice and toast, tossing frequently, for 3 minutes or until the rice turns golden. Tip the rice into a pestle and mortar, or grinder, and pound until roughly ground. Set aside.

3 Pour the oil into the hot wok or pan and add the shallots, the white parts of the spring onions, the lemongrass, ginger and garlic, and half the chilli and stir-fry for 2 minutes. Next, add the mince and stir-fry, breaking it up as you cook, for another 5 minutes, until evenly browned.

4 Drain the noodles and add them to the wok. Turn the heat down to medium and pour in 4 tablespoons of water, the fish sauce and the lime juice. Add the sugar and, using tongs, turn until everything is combined and heated through. Remove from the heat and stir in the ground rice, herbs and remaining chilli. Season with salt and pepper, to taste.

5 Arrange the lettuce leaves in four large shallow serving bowls and top with the pork noodles. Scatter over the peanuts and reserved green parts of the spring onions before serving with extra wedges of lime.

# SRIRACHA HOR FUN NOODLES

This is one of the most famous vegetarian dishes to originate from the Phuket Jay Festival, the island equivalent of the Bangkok Jay Festival (see page 60). It is a delicious combination of stir-fried sticky rice noodles and fresh garden vegetables blended with ginger and the spiciness and the sourness of sriracha sauce.

**SERVES** 4
**PREP** 10 minutes
**COOK** 15 minutes

200g/7oz hor fun noodles (wide rice noodles), separated into individual strands before cooking
3 tablespoons vegetable oil
60g/2¼oz button mushrooms, cut in half
5 garlic cloves, finely chopped
1 small onion, thinly sliced
1 red pepper, seeds removed and thinly sliced diagonally
60g/2¼oz shimeji mushrooms, trimmed
30g/1oz spinach leaves, tough stalks removed
1 spring onion, thinly sliced diagonally
2.5cm/1in piece of root ginger, peeled and finely grated
3 tablespoons light soy sauce
3 tablespoons sriracha sauce

1 First, cook the noodles following the instructions on the packet, then drain and refresh under cold running water. Return the noodles to the pan, cover with cold water and set aside.

2 Heat a large wok or frying pan over a high heat. Add the oil and when hot, add the button mushrooms and stir-fry for 3 minutes, until tender.

3 Add the garlic, onion, red pepper and shimeji mushrooms and stir-fry for 3 minutes.

4 Drain the noodles and add them to the wok or pan with the spinach, spring onion, ginger, light soy sauce and sriracha sauce and toss gently and continuously for another 2 minutes, until golden and heated through. Remove from the heat and allow to rest for 1 minute before serving.

Phuket is now one of the most popular tourist destinations in Thailand. A noble island, with a rich tin-mining history, it became a Thai state in the 13th century, and in the 1500s provided a safe stop-off for ships on trading routes between China and India. In the 17th century, two women – Lady Chan and Lady Muk – rallied the islanders to see off a siege by Burmese invaders aiming to conquer Thailand (then Siam). Honoured by the Thai king, they earned themselves the name 'The Two Heroines'.

# FRIED RICE

Thais will eat fried rice, a popular street-food staple, at any time of the day, breakfast included. Thrown together with the minimum fuss or effort, fried rice is quick and filling and is a great way to use up any leftovers. Most fried-rice dishes are made using cooked jasmine rice, a long-grain, fragrant variety most commonly associated with Thai food. You need to travel only a short distance out of the hectic bustle of Bangkok to see how important rice is to local communities. Farmers still honour the ancient Rice Goddess or Rice Mother, Mae Phosop, and their beliefs influence all stages of rice growing, from sowing and tending to eventual harvesting and threshing. When Thais invite guests to dinner, they often say 'come and have rice with us'. This reverence dates back several hundred years, when an abundance of rice (and fish) was a measure of happiness and prosperity, hence the saying 'There are fish in the water, there is rice in the fields...'.

The notion of wasting food is alien to Thai culture, so leftover cooked rice is rarely thrown away. For the best fried rice, use rice that has been left to cool completely after cooking (fried warm rice turns into a soggy mess) – day-old cooked rice is best of all. If you're cooking your rice specifically to fry (rather than using leftover), it's best to use slightly less water than normal (see page 259) as you want the grain to hold its shape. To speed up the cooling process, spread the cooked grains out on a large platter so that the moisture can evaporate and to prevent any bacterial growth. Once cooled, put the rice in a sealed container and store it in the fridge until you're ready to use it.

For the best results when stir-frying, heat the dry wok and then add the oil. Heat the oil and swirl it around and then add the flavourings, followed by your choice of protein and/or vegetables. The rice comes next – resist the urge to stir it. Instead toss it frequently with a wok ladle or spatula until it is thoroughly heated through to piping hot and even in colour, and you have broken up any lumps. You should almost hear the rice pop or crack in the pan while you cook it. For the finishing touch, the classic way to serve fried rice is with fish sauce combined with chopped chillies and a wedge of lime.

## ⓥ ASPARAGUS FRIED RICE

Fried rice is typical Thai street food. It's a perfect way to use up leftover cooked rice, but make sure the rice is cold before you start so the grains remain separate when stir-fried, and that you reheat it thoroughly until piping hot. This egg-fried rice is particularly flavourful with the sweetness of the apple and sun-dried tomato and the earthiness of the asparagus. It's best cooked quickly over a high heat to help caramelize the rice a little.

**SERVES** 4
**PREP** 10 minutes
**COOK** 10 minutes

3 tablespoons vegetable oil
4 garlic cloves, roughly chopped
2 eggs, lightly beaten
50g/1¾oz sun-dried tomatoes in oil, drained and cut in half
1 green apple, peeled, cored and diced
10 asparagus stalks, trimmed and sliced
500g/1lb 2oz cooked cold jasmine rice (about 185g/6½oz uncooked weight)
2 tablespoons light soy sauce
1 lime, cut into quarters

1  Heat a large wok or frying pan over a high heat. Add the oil and garlic and stir-fry for 1 minute without letting it colour. Add the eggs and cook, stirring continuously, for 2 minutes or until scrambled and firm.

2  Add the sun-dried tomatoes, apple and asparagus and stir-fry for 3 minutes before adding the rice.

3  Using a wok ladle, flip the rice to keep it moving, then add the soy sauce and cook for 3 minutes, until the rice is golden and thoroughly heated through. Leave the rice to rest for 1 minute, then serve in bowls with wedges of lime on the side.

# CHILLI PRAWN FRIED RICE

This Busaba favourite is an adaption of a chilli prawn stir-fry with the addition of jasmine rice to make a complete dish. You can find chilli jam paste in Asian grocers or online.

**SERVES** 4
**PREP** 15 minutes
**COOK** 10 minutes

3 tablespoons vegetable oil
4 garlic cloves, roughly chopped
16 raw peeled king or tiger prawns, deveined
1 Thai red chilli, sliced diagonally
1 Thai green chilli, sliced diagonally
4 kaffir lime leaves, shredded
6 shiitake mushrooms, thinly sliced
1 small onion, thinly sliced
3 tablespoons Chilli Jam (see page 258) or shop-bought Thai chilli jam paste
2 tablespoons fish sauce
1 tablespoon oyster sauce
10 Thai basil leaves or regular basil
500g/1lb 2oz cooked cold jasmine rice (about 185g/6½oz uncooked rice)
1 lime, cut into quarters

1  Heat a large wok or frying pan over a high heat. Add the oil and garlic and stir-fry for 1 minute without letting the garlic colour. Add the prawns, both types of chilli, the kaffir lime leaves, the shiitake mushrooms and the onion and stir-fry for 2 minutes, or until the prawns are cooked through.

2  Stir in the chilli jam, fish sauce and oyster sauce and continue to stir-fry for another minute. Add the basil and 3 tablespoons of water, followed by the rice.

3  Using a wok ladle, flip the rice to keep it moving and cook for 3 minutes, until golden and thoroughly heated through. Leave the dish to rest for 1 minute, then serve in bowls with wedges of lime on the side.

Although many people assume jasmine rice is so-called because of its fragrant, floral nature, in fact it is a reference to its pure whiteness, like the jasmine flower. In Thai culture, the jasmine flower has come to symbolize the pure love felt by a mother towards her children.

# EGG-FRIED RICE BOWL WITH PARSNIP CRISPS

**At Busaba, we sometimes serve parsnip crisps as a snack on their own, but they are also a delicious and easy way to add a bit of crunch and contrast in texture to a fried rice, albeit a twist on tradition.**

**SERVES** 4
**PREP** 15 minutes
**COOK** 15 minutes

2 tablespoons light soy sauce
1 tablespoon fish sauce, plus extra
    to serve
1 teaspoon palm sugar or light soft
    brown sugar
4 spring onions, white and green
    parts separated, thinly sliced
1 red pepper, deseeded and
    chopped
85g/3oz green cabbage, shredded
3 garlic cloves, finely chopped
2 Thai red chillies, deseeded and
    thinly sliced
570g/1lb 4½oz cooked cold jasmine
    rice, preferably brown (about
    200g/7oz uncooked rice)
3 eggs, lightly beaten
a large handful coriander leaves,
    chopped
1 lime, cut into quarters, to serve
salt and freshly ground black
    pepper

**FOR THE PARSNIP CRISPS**
vegetable oil, for deep-frying
2 parsnips, peeled and sliced into
    thin strips using a vegetable
    peeler

1 First, make the parsnip crisps. Pour enough oil into a large wok (use a wok stand to keep the pan stable), saucepan or deep-fat fryer to deep-fry the parsnips. Heat the oil to 180°C/350°F or until a cube of day-old bread turns crisp and golden in 45 seconds. Add a small handful of the parsnip ribbons, use a fork to separate the strands and fry for 1 minute or until light golden and crisp – do not let them become too dark or they will turn bitter. Drain the parsnip crisps on kitchen paper and repeat until all the parsnips are cooked. Set aside, turn off the heat and reserve the oil you've used for frying.

2 Mix together the soy sauce, fish sauce and sugar and set aside.

3 Pour off all but 2 tablespoons of the parsnip frying oil and set the wok or pan over a high heat. Add the white part of the spring onions, the red pepper and the cabbage and stir-fry for 1 minute, until the vegetables are starting to soften. Add the garlic and half the chilli slices and stir-fry for another minute.

4 Add the rice and stir-fry until thoroughly heated through and piping hot. Push the rice to one side of the wok and add the eggs to the empty side. Stir the eggs and when they start to set and scramble, fold them into the rice. Continue to stir-fry until the eggs are fully cooked. Add the soy sauce mixture and the green parts of the spring onions and give everything a quick stir. Season with salt and pepper, to taste.

5 Spoon the rice into large shallow bowls and scatter over the coriander and remaining chilli. Top with the parsnip crisps and serve with wedges of lime, and extra fish sauce, if you like.

# CHILLI BEEF JASMINE RICE

**This classic Thai street-food dish comes in all manner of variations. It is usually hot and spicy with pork, chicken or a fried egg served on top. This version is slightly different to the chilli beef we serve up in the restaurants, but wonderfully delicious for making at home.**

**SERVES** 4
**PREP** 20 minutes
**COOK** 10 minutes

2 tablespoons vegetable oil
400g/14oz beef mince
400g/14oz cooked cold jasmine rice (about 150g/5½oz uncooked weight)
1 Thai red chilli, halved or sliced diagonally
1 Thai green chilli, halved or sliced diagonally
1 tablespoon fish sauce
½ teaspoon caster sugar
1 tablespoon oyster sauce
15 Thai basil leaves or regular basil

**FOR THE CHILLI PASTE**
4 garlic cloves, roughly chopped
1 Thai red chilli, roughly chopped
1 Thai green chilli, roughly chopped
a pinch of salt

**FOR THE NAM PLA PRIK (CHILLI FISH SAUCE)**
1 small red Thai chilli, finely chopped
1 small Thai green chilli, finely chopped
juice of ¼ lime
2 tablespoons fish sauce

1  First, make the chilli paste. Put the garlic, both types of chilli and a pinch of salt in a pestle and mortar and pound until it forms a paste. Alternatively, use a mini food processor or grinder. Set aside.

2  To make the nam pla prik, mix together all the ingredients in a small bowl, then set aside.

3  Heat a large wok or frying pan over a high heat. Add the oil and when hot, add the beef and stir-fry for 3 minutes, until browned. Stir in the prepared chilli paste and stir-fry for 2 minutes, until you can smell the aroma of the paste, then add the rice.

4  Using a wok ladle, flip the rice to keep it moving, then add both types of chilli, the fish sauce, sugar, oyster sauce and 2 tablespoons of water and continue to cook over a high heat for 3 minutes, until golden and thoroughly heated through. Stir in the basil and leave to rest for 1 minute, then serve in bowls with the nam pla prik sauce on the side.

# FEAST

# CURRY

Thai curries are quite different from those in India and other Southeast Asian countries. Most rely on fresh herbs and spices with dried spices playing a supporting, rather than a title role. They range from the simple to the complex with every region having its own particular flavour combinations and nuances. From the north comes jungle curry, which unlike many other Thai curries doesn't contain coconut milk, allowing the flavour of the herbs and spices to dominate. From the south there's massaman, a rich and flavourful coconut-based curry with warming flavours of cardamom, cloves and cinnamon.

Red and green curries are the most well-known Thai curries outside Thailand. While the origins of the former are unclear, the hotter of the two – green curry – originates from the central plains. Both are certainly more southern than northern, where coconut milk – which forms the basis for both – is less often used in cooking (because the northern climate is less suited to coconut growing).

At the heart of a Thai curry is the paste. This specific combination of herbs, spices and seasonings gives a characteristic balance of flavours and nuances. (See page 253 for more on curry pastes.) Fragrant and aromatic galangal, lemongrass, kaffir lime leaves, krachai (wild ginger) and coriander roots are all familiar, not forgetting chilli with its unmissable heat. If dried spices feature, coriander seeds and cumin seeds are most common and are roasted in a dry frying pan until fragrant before grinding into the paste.

While a paste is the core of a Thai curry, how you cook it and the other ingredients that you add provide the finishing touches. Make sure you buy the right cut of meat or type of fish for your dish. For example, avoid using cuts of meat that require long, slow cooking in a curry that takes minutes to make (you'll be left with too much chewiness if you do); and fish has a tendency to fall apart, so you need a slightly firm, meaty fish (such as sea bass or red mullet) that holds its shape in a fish curry.

# GREEN CHICKEN CURRY

A typical Thai green curry has a distinctive consistency – most obviously, it is much thinner than East Asian curries. The main ingredients of the curry paste are fresh aromatic Thai herbs and spicy fresh chillies. There are lots of good ready-made pastes on the market these days, but we think there's no substitute for making your own, if you have time.

**SERVES** 4
**PREP** 15 minutes
**COOK** 25 minutes

2 tablespoons vegetable oil
150g/5½oz Green Curry Paste (see page 254) or ready-made paste
a pinch of salt
500ml/17fl oz coconut milk
2 boneless, skinless chicken breasts, cut horizontally through the middle, then cut into 5mm/¼in thick slices
30g/1oz pea aubergines
2 Thai aubergines, each cut into 4 wedges
½–1 Thai red chilli, sliced diagonally, to taste
½–1 Thai green chilli, sliced diagonally, to taste
5 kaffir lime leaves
2 tablespoons fish sauce
30g/1oz palm sugar or light soft brown sugar
8 Thai basil leaves or regular basil leaves

1  Heat a large wok or heavy-based saucepan over a medium heat. Add the oil and stir in the green curry paste and salt. Cook, stirring, for 2 minutes, then add half of the coconut milk and simmer for 5 minutes, until the oil floats to the top and the sauce turns green in colour.

2  Add the chicken, pea aubergines, Thai aubergines, both types of chilli and the kaffir lime leaves and cook for 1 minute, stirring regularly. Stir in the remaining coconut milk and 4 tablespoons of water. Bring to the boil, then reduce the heat and stir in the fish sauce and sugar and simmer for 15 minutes, until the chicken is cooked.

3  Remove the curry from the heat and add the basil. Serve in individual portions, or in one or two large serving bowls for everyone to help themselves, with jasmine rice on the side.

# BEEF CHEEK JUNGLE CURRY

Thai red curry paste with the addition of lemongrass and krachai (wild ginger) are at the heart of a jungle curry, which originates from the north of Thailand. Unlike red and green curries, jungle curry doesn't feature coconut milk so it's not creamy and this allows the true flavour of the fresh herbs and spices to come through. Beef cheeks require long, slow cooking to become meltingly tender – if you can't find them, use braising beef or stewing steak instead.

**SERVES** 4
**PREP** 20 minutes, plus soaking
**COOK** 1 hour 40 minutes

40g/1½oz dried shiitake mushrooms, broken into bite-sized pieces
300ml/10½fl oz just-boiled hot water
1 tablespoon rapeseed oil
4 garlic cloves, finely chopped
3 tablespoons Red Curry Paste (see page 254) or ready-made paste
1 lemongrass stick, bruised
2 teaspoons finely chopped krachai (wild ginger; optional)
750g/1lb 10oz beef cheeks, trimmed of excess fat and cut into 2cm/¾in chunks
500ml/17fl oz beef stock
2 tablespoons fish sauce
1 teaspoon palm sugar or light soft brown sugar
3 kaffir lime leaves
3 carrots, sliced diagonally, about 5mm/¼in thick
85g/3oz green beans, trimmed and cut in half
40g/1½oz cashew nuts, ground
2 spring onions, cut diagonally, to serve
a handful basil leaves, to serve
salt and ground white pepper

1 Put the dried shiitake in a heatproof bowl and pour over the hot water. Cover the bowl and leave to soak for 20 minutes, until softened. Drain, reserving the soaking liquid, and discard any tough stalks.

2 Heat a large lidded wok or heavy-based saucepan over a medium–high heat. Add the oil, garlic, curry paste, lemongrass and krachai, if using, and stir-fry for 1 minute. Add the beef, stir until the meat is coated in the aromatics, then fry, turning occasionally, for 5 minutes, until the meat is browned all over.

3 Pour in the stock, strained mushroom soaking liquid and fish sauce, then stir in the sugar, kaffir lime leaves and hydrated shiitake. Bring the liquid to the boil, then reduce the heat to low, cover with a lid and simmer for 1 hour.

4 Add the carrots, green beans and ground cashews and cook, covered, for another 30 minutes, until the beef and vegetables are tender. If there is too much liquid, remove the lid and let the sauce reduce and thicken. Alternatively, add a splash of water if it is too dry.

5 Season the curry with salt and pepper to taste, then spoon into one or two serving bowls, sprinkle with the spring onions and basil leaves, and bring to the table with bowls of jasmine rice for everyone to help themselves.

v vg gf n 🌶🌶

# PUMPKIN GREEN CURRY

**We have created this dish for our vegetarian fans who love green curry. The sweetness of the vegetables makes the curry milder than a meat or fish version, but all the fresh herbs make it wonderfully aromatic to make up for the lost heat.**

**SERVES** 4
**PREP** 15 minutes
**COOK** 25 minutes

2 tablespoons vegetable oil
150g/5½oz Green Curry Paste
    (see page 254 – leave out the
    shrimp paste if vegetarian) or
    ready-made paste
500ml/17fl oz coconut milk
400g/14oz pumpkin, peeled,
    deseeded and cut into
    3cm/1¼in dice
100g/3½oz canned bamboo shoots,
    drained and thinly sliced
2 tablespoons pea aubergines
5 kaffir lime leaves, torn
½ Thai red chilli, sliced diagonally
½ Thai green chilli, sliced
    diagonally
30g/1oz palm sugar or light soft
    brown sugar
1 teaspoon salt
8 Thai basil leaves or regular basil

1  Heat a large wok or heavy-based saucepan over a medium heat. Add the oil and stir in the green curry paste. Cook, stirring, for 2 minutes, then add half of the coconut milk and simmer for 5 minutes, until the oil floats to the top and the sauce turns green in colour.

2  Add the pumpkin, bamboo shoots, pea aubergines, kaffir lime leaves and both types of chilli and cook for 1 minute, stirring regularly. Stir in the remaining coconut milk and 4 tablespoons of water. Bring the liquid to the boil, then reduce the heat to low and stir in the sugar and salt. Simmer for 15 minutes, until the pumpkin is tender.

3  Remove the curry from heat and stir in the basil. Serve in individual portions, or in one or two large serving bowls for everyone to help themselves, with jasmine rice on the side.

gf n ▸

# RED MULLET CURRY

This is a curry sauce made for sipping – thin, with fresh pineapple that gives sweetness to the already delicious combination of salty, sour and mildly spicy flavours. We're certain you'll keep coming back to taste some more...

**SERVES** 4
**PREP** 15 minutes
**COOK** 25 minutes

200g/7oz ripe pineapple, skin and core removed
3 tablespoons vegetable oil
4 tablespoons Red Curry Paste (see page 254) or ready-made paste
½ teaspoon ground coriander
500ml/17fl oz coconut milk
4 kaffir lime leaves, torn
1 tablespoon fish sauce
40g/1½oz palm sugar or light soft brown sugar
1 tablespoon tamarind concentrate or paste
8 red mullet fillets
chaplu leaves or Thai basil leaves or regular basil, to serve
2 whole dried chillies, toasted (see page 83), to serve

1  Thinly slice half of the pineapple into 3cm/1¼in long slices, then finely chop the remaining pineapple. Set aside.

2  Heat a large wok or heavy-based saucepan over a medium heat. Add the oil and when hot, stir in the red curry paste and ground coriander. Cook, stirring, for 2 minutes, then add half of the coconut milk and simmer for 5 minutes, until the oil floats to the top and the sauce turns reddish in colour.

3  Stir in the remaining coconut milk and 200ml/7fl oz of water and bring to the boil. Reduce the heat to low and stir in the sliced and chopped pineapple, kaffir lime leaves, fish sauce, sugar and tamarind, then simmer for 10 minutes, stirring occasionally. Arrange the red mullet fillets in the wok or pan, spoon the sauce over and simmer for another 5 minutes, until the fish is cooked through.

4  Remove the curry from the heat and bring to the table in individual portions, or one or two large serving bowls, sprinkled with chaplu or basil leaves and with the toasted dried chilli crumbled over the top. Serve with jasmine rice.

# SONGKHLA BEEF CURRY

Songkhla is a southern Thai province, not far from Malaysia. Its heavy Malaysian influences have been adapted to Thai taste buds with the addition of spice and it is a firm favourite on the Busaba menu. You can braise the beef up to a day in advance.

**SERVES** 4
**PREP** 10 minutes, plus brisket braising time (about 2½ hours)
**COOK** 25–30 minutes

3 tablespoons vegetable oil
120g/4¼oz Songkhla Curry Paste (see page 256) or ready-made paste
500ml/17fl oz coconut milk
4 Thai red chillies, chopped
270g/9½oz cherry tomatoes, halve 5 of the tomatoes and chop the rest
1 teaspoon dried Turkish Aleppo pepper or dried mild chilli flakes
2 tablespoons fish sauce
15g/½oz palm sugar or light soft brown sugar
2 spring onions, finely sliced, to serve

**FOR THE BRAISED BRISKET**
1kg/2lb 4oz beef brisket, trimmed and cut into 3cm/1¼in cubes
30g/1oz salt
30g/1oz cracked black peppercorns
1 teaspoon coriander seeds, toasted (see page 32)
5 coriander stalks
1 onion, cut into 8 wedges
55g/2oz caster sugar

1 First, braise the brisket. Rub the beef with the salt and place it in a large saucepan. Put the cracked black peppercorns and the coriander seeds in a small muslin spice bag, so they are easy to pick out at the end of the cooking time, then add to the pan with the coriander stalks, onion and sugar. Pour in 2 litres/70fl oz of water and bring the liquid to the boil. Reduce the heat, cover and simmer for 2½ hours, until the brisket is tender. Remove the pan from the heat and strain the brisket, discarding the muslin bag, coriander stalks, onion and cooking water.

2 When you're ready to make the curry, heat a large wok or heavy-based saucepan over a medium heat. Add the oil and stir in the songkhla curry paste. Cook, stirring, for 2 minutes, then add half of the coconut milk and simmer for 5 minutes, until the oil floats to the top and the sauce turns reddish in colour.

3 Stir in the remaining coconut milk and 150ml/5fl oz of water. Bring the liquid to the boil, then reduce the heat to low and stir in the red chillies, the halved and chopped tomatoes, the chilli pepper or flakes, fish sauce, sugar and cooked brisket. Simmer the curry, stirring occasionally, for 20 minutes, until reduced and thickened.

4 Remove the curry from the heat and bring to the table in individual portions, or one or two large serving bowls, sprinkled with the sliced spring onions. Serve with jasmine rice on the side.

# AROMATIC SPICED CHICKEN CURRY

Known in Thai as *gang gari gai*, this is a famous Thai–Muslim fusion recipe that has variations all over Southeast Asia. The main ingredient of the curry paste is turmeric, giving the curry a glorious yellow colour.

**SERVES** 4
**PREP** 15 minutes
**COOK** 40 minutes

3 tablespoons vegetable oil
150g/5½oz Yellow Curry Paste (see page 255) or ready-made paste
500ml/17fl oz coconut milk
3 boneless, skinless chicken breasts, about 600g/1lb 5oz total weight, cut into 3cm/1¼in pieces
2 potatoes, such as Maris Piper, peeled and cut into 3cm/1¼in cubes
2 tablespoons fish sauce
50g/1¾oz palm sugar or light soft brown sugar
1 pandan leaf (optional)
1 teaspoon salt
1 tablespoon Golden Fried Shallots (see page 258) or ready-made crispy fried shallots, to serve
Cucumber Relish (see page 32), to serve

1  Heat a large wok or heavy-based saucepan over a medium heat. Add the oil and stir in the yellow curry paste. Cook, stirring, for 6–8 minutes, until the paste smells aromatic. Add half of the coconut milk and simmer for 5 minutes, until the oil floats to the top and the sauce turns yellow in colour.

2  Add the chicken and potatoes and cook for 3 minutes, stirring regularly. Stir in the remaining coconut milk and 4 tablespoons of water. Bring to the boil, then reduce the heat and stir in the fish sauce, sugar, pandan leaf, if using, and salt and simmer for 20 minutes, until the chicken and potatoes are cooked.

3  Remove the curry from the heat and bring to the table in individual portions, or in one or two large serving bowls, with the fried shallots scattered over the top. Serve with the cucumber relish and jasmine rice on the side.

In Thai cooking, fried shallot is mostly used as a topping to give the dish a sweet but savoury aroma. You'll find that the oil left after frying the shallots is beautifully perfumed – save it if you can, and use it for cooking stir-fries.

# LAMB & PUMPKIN MASSAMAN CURRY

Slow-cooked until incredibly tender, the lamb in this curry is combined with golden pumpkin and new potatoes, and topped off with peanuts, which add a bit of crunch. Massaman is a fragrant, rich curry from the south of Thailand. The pumpkin is an unusual addition, but it adds a lovely touch of colour. Use butternut squash if pumpkin is out of season.

**SERVES** 4
**PREP** 15 minutes
**COOK** 1¾ hours

1 tablespoon rapeseed oil
650g/1lb 7oz diced lean lamb
    shoulder or neck
1 large onion, roughly chopped
5cm/2in piece of root ginger, peeled
    and finely chopped
3 garlic cloves, finely chopped
3 tablespoons Massaman
    Curry Paste (see page 255) or
    ready-made paste
400ml/14fl oz coconut milk
455ml/16fl oz lamb stock
1 tablespoon fish sauce
1 teaspoon palm sugar or light soft
    brown sugar
3 kaffir lime leaves
200g/7oz new potatoes, such as
    Charlotte, halved or quartered
    if large
500g/1lb 2 oz pumpkin, skin and
    seeds removed, cut into bite-
    sized chunks
a handful coriander leaves,
    chopped, plus extra to serve
4 tablespoons roughly chopped
    roasted unsalted peanuts
salt and ground white pepper

1 Heat a large lidded wok or heavy-based saucepan over a medium heat. Add the oil and when hot, add the lamb and cook for 5 minutes or until browned all over. (You may need to do this in two batches.) Remove the lamb from the wok or pan and set aside. Add the onion and stir-fry for another 5 minutes, until softened. Stir in the ginger, garlic and curry paste and cook for 2 minutes. Return the lamb to the wok or pan.

2 Pour in the coconut milk, stock and fish sauce, then stir in the sugar and kaffir lime leaves. Bring to the boil, then turn the heat down to low, cover and simmer for 1 hour, stirring occasionally.

3 Add the new potatoes, pumpkin and coriander, replace the lid and cook for another 20–30 minutes, until the vegetables and lamb are tender. If there is too much liquid, remove the lid and let the sauce reduce and thicken. Alternatively, add a splash of water if it is too dry.

4 Season the curry with salt and pepper, to taste, then scatter over the peanuts and extra coriander. Transfer to individual bowls or one or two large serving bowls and serve with jasmine rice.

# WOK STIR-FRY & MORE

Central to the Thai kitchen, a wok is more than just a pan for stir-frying; it's also an incredibly versatile piece of kitchen kit. Steamed, deep-fried, braised and even smoked dishes are all as doable in a wok as the classic stir-fry.

You'll certainly get a taste for how adaptable this simple pan is in this chapter of wok-cooked recipes, which includes everything from duck breasts smoked over jasmine rice (see page 147) and a Chinese-influenced Thai Sweet & Sour Chicken (see page 139) to Ginger Beef (see page 142) and a chilli venison stir-fry (see page 138).

Although all woks are fundamentally the same, you do need to consider material, size and shape when buying one. If cooking for four people, you need a large wok – and you'll get better results if you use a large wok, rather than cook with an overcrowded smaller one. A large surface area will help to cook the food quickly and evenly. Similarly, a wok with a single long handle is better than one with no handle, as it distances you from any stray spitting oil. Two-handled woks, however, tend to be more stable and are better for dishes that contain a sauce, as well as those that are deep-fried or steamed.

If you have a gas hob then a round-bottomed wok is ideal for stir-frying as its shape allows the heat to spread evenly up the sides of the pan for speedy, even cooking, but it's a good idea to use a wok stand to keep the pan stable. Flat-bottomed woks are perfect for electric or induction hobs as they are in direct contact with the heat source and don't wobble about.

The best modern woks are said to be made with carbon steel, which is a good heat conductor and is non-stick when seasoned properly. You need to season your wok when you first buy it and at regular intervals to keep it in good condition. To do this, pour in 2 tablespoons of a mild-tasting cooking oil, such as sunflower oil, and rub it all over using a scrunched up piece of kitchen paper. Place the wok over a low heat for 10–15 minutes, then wipe the inside of the wok again with more paper. Repeat the heating and wiping process until the kitchen paper comes away clean. A well-seasoned wok is highly prized in Asia: not only will it last much longer than one left to its own devices, it won't rust and in time becomes non-stick, imparting your food with a slight smokiness that immediately transports you to the streets of Bangkok.

# PORK WITH SNAKE BEANS
# IN YELLOW BEAN SAUCE

Snake beans, also known as yard-long beans, are long, thin green beans that are popular in Asian cooking. When buying the beans, make sure that they are firm and crisp; they should snap easily when broken, rather than be wobbly and soft. If you can't find them, use fine green beans instead. Yellow bean sauce is made from fermented soya beans and, despite its name, is brown rather than yellow in colour. It lends a rich, intense flavour to stir-fries and marinades.

**SERVES** 4
**PREP** 15 minutes, plus marinating
**COOK** 15 minutes

2 tablespoons rapeseed oil
4 tablespoons yellow bean sauce
2 tablespoons tamarind
    concentrate or paste
550g/1lb 4oz pork loin, membrane
    removed and excess fat
    trimmed, cut into large
    bite-sized chunks
2 teaspoons coriander seeds
3 banana shallots, thinly sliced
2 large garlic cloves, thinly sliced
1 Thai red chilli, thinly sliced into
    rings
2.5cm/1in piece of root ginger,
    peeled and cut into matchsticks
1 teaspoon palm sugar or light soft
    brown sugar
125g/4½oz snake beans or fine
    green beans, trimmed and cut
    into 2.5cm/1in lengths
225g/8oz can bamboo shoots,
    drained (about 140g/5oz drained
    weight)
3 spring onions, thinly sliced
    diagonally, to serve
salt and ground white pepper

1  Mix together half the oil with the yellow bean sauce and the tamarind concentrate or paste in a large shallow dish. Add the pork and turn to coat it in the marinade. Cover and leave the pork to marinate for 1 hour, or overnight in the fridge, if you have time.

2  Put the coriander seeds in a large wok or frying pan and toast them over a medium heat for 1 minute or until they start to smell aromatic. Tip them into a pestle and mortar and grind to a powder. Alternatively, use a mini food processor or grinder.

3  Return the wok or pan to a high heat and add the remaining oil. Using a slotted spoon, lift the pork out of the marinade and stir-fry for 3 minutes, until browned. (Reserve the marinade for later.) Add the shallots, garlic, chilli and ginger and stir-fry for another 2 minutes.

4  Reduce the heat to medium, add 150ml/5fl oz of water, then the sugar, snake or green beans, bamboo shoots, ground coriander seeds and reserved marinade. Cook, stirring often, for 5 minutes or until the beans are tender. Add a splash more water if the stir-fry needs more sauce.

5  Season the stir-fry with salt and white pepper, to taste, and serve sprinkled with spring onions.

# GOLDEN SEA BASS IN GINGER TAMARIND SAUCE

Tamarind has a memorable, sour taste that works really well with seafood, but you do need the addition of sugar to balance it out. This recipe makes use of tamarind paste, which can simply be spooned out of a jar or tub and doesn't need any preparation. You could make the sauce ahead of serving and reheat it before use.

**SERVES** 4
**PREP** 20 minutes
**COOK** 20 minutes

4 large sea bass fillets, pin-boned
plain flour, for coating
a handful chopped coriander leaves
    and Golden Fried Ginger and
    Golden Fried Garlic (see page
    258), to serve
salt and freshly ground black
    pepper

**FOR THE GINGER TAMARIND SAUCE**
2 large garlic cloves
4cm/1½in piece of root ginger,
    peeled and roughly chopped
4 large vine-ripened tomatoes,
    cut in half and deseeded
1 tablespoon groundnut oil, plus
    extra for frying the sea bass
1 teaspoon palm sugar or light soft
    brown sugar
3 tablespoons tamarind
    concentrate or paste
1 Thai red chilli, deseeded and
    finely chopped
1 tablespoon fish sauce

1  First prepare the ginger tamarind sauce. Blitz the garlic, ginger and tomatoes in a blender or mini food processor until almost smooth. Heat the oil in a large wok or frying pan over a medium heat. Add the tomato mixture and 3 tablespoons of water and heat almost to boiling point. Stir in the sugar, tamarind, chilli and fish sauce, reduce the heat to low and simmer for 5 minutes, until the liquid has reduced and thickened slightly. Pour the sauce into a bowl, then wipe the wok or pan clean using kitchen paper. Set aside.

2  Cut each sea bass fillet in half lengthways and pat dry with kitchen paper. Generously coat a serving plate with flour and season well with salt and pepper.

3  Pour enough oil to fill a wok or pan by 2cm/¾in and heat over a high heat. When hot, turn the heat down to medium. Dust each strip of sea bass in the seasoned flour and carefully lower it into the hot oil. Fry the fish in batches – you'll probably fit about 3–4 strips in the wok or pan at a time – for about 5 minutes, turning once, until golden. Scoop out the fish using a fish slice and allow each batch to drain on kitchen paper while you fry the remaining fish.

4  When all the fish strips are cooked, pour off the oil and return the sauce to the wok or pan. Reheat the sauce briefly, then place spoonfuls of the sauce on a serving plate, arrange the fish on top and scatter over the coriander and golden fried ginger and garlic. Bring to the table and allow everyone to help themselves to strips of the fried fish with a drizzling of sauce over.

# SWEET CHILLI AUBERGINE WITH COCONUT RICE

**The aubergine in this recipe is cooked until melt-in-the-mouth tender and served in a fiery chilli–ginger sauce. Cooling coconut rice and a scattering of fragrant Thai basil leaves add balance.**

**SERVES** 4
**PREP** 15 minutes
**COOK** 25 minutes

4 tablespoons rapeseed oil
2 aubergines, cut into 1cm/½in thick slices and halved or quartered, if large
3 banana shallots, thinly sliced into rings
4 garlic cloves, finely chopped
5cm/2in piece of root ginger, peeled and finely chopped
2 tablespoons light soy sauce
1 tablespoon fish sauce (or lime juice for vegetarians and vegans)
3 tablespoons Sweet Chilli Sauce (see page 257) or sriracha sauce
juice of ½ lime
a handful Thai basil leaves or regular basil, plus extra to serve
Coconut Rice (see page 259), to serve
salt and freshly ground black pepper

1  Heat a large wok or frying pan over a high heat. Add the oil and when hot, add the aubergines and stir-fry for 8–10 minutes, until they have softened and released their oil. Reduce the heat to medium, add the shallots, garlic and ginger and stir-fry for another 2 minutes.

2  Add the soy sauce, fish sauce, sweet chilli or sriracha sauce and 250ml/9fl oz of water and simmer over a medium–low heat, stirring occasionally, for another 10 minutes, until the aubergine is tender and the sauce becomes glossy.

3  Stir in the lime juice and basil leaves and season with salt and pepper, to taste. Serve the aubergine with coconut rice and a few extra basil leaves scattered over the top.

> Initially it may look as though there isn't enough oil in the wok when you cook the aubergine, but be patient... it will happen. To make this dish vegetarian, substitute the fish sauce with the same quantity of lime juice, and use sriracha sauce rather than sweet chilli sauce.

# CHILLI VENISON

This is a dish where East meets West. Venison – lean and flavourful – is tenderized with tamarind paste and spiced during cooking with Thai chilli and Padrón peppers (the latter from northwestern Spain). It's fusion at its delicious best.

**SERVES** 4
**PREP** 10 minutes, plus marinating
**COOK** 5 minutes

400g/14oz venison loin, trimmed and cut into 3cm/1¼in cubes
1 tablespoon tamarind concentrate or paste
3 tablespoons vegetable oil
55g/2oz whole Padrón peppers or small green peppers
5 garlic cloves, finely chopped
1 Thai red chilli, thinly sliced diagonally
1 yellow or red pepper, deseeded and sliced diagonally
55g/2oz sugar snap peas
a pinch of dried chilli flakes
2 tablespoons fish sauce
a pinch of caster sugar
2 tablespoons oyster sauce

1  Put the venison in a medium mixing bowl, add the tamarind and turn until coated all over. Cover and leave to marinate for 2 hours.

2  Heat a large wok or frying pan over a high heat. Add the oil and when very hot, add the venison and stir-fry for 2 minutes, until well browned. Add the Padrón peppers or bell peppers, along with the garlic, chilli, red pepper and sugar snaps, and stir-fry for another 1 minute.

3  Add the chilli flakes, fish sauce, sugar, oyster sauce and 3 tablespoons of water, then heat through briefly. Remove the wok or pan from the heat and allow to rest for 1 minute before transferring to a platter and serving immediately.

# THAI SWEET & SOUR CHICKEN

**This fried crispy chicken, tossed in a sweet-and-sour sauce, is a staple lunch dish in Bangkok. Sourness comes from the tamarind and the sweetness comes from the pineapple.**

**SERVES** 4–6
**PREP** 20 minutes
**COOK** 30 minutes

50g/1¾oz plain flour
50g/1¾oz cornflour
2 pinches of salt
2 pinches of ground white pepper
800g/1lb 12oz chicken breasts, cut into 3cm/1¼in cubes
250ml/9fl oz vegetable oil, plus extra if needed
1 onion, finely sliced
180g/6¼oz cherry tomatoes, halved or quartered if large
2 Thai red chillies, thinly sliced diagonally
2 Thai green chillies, thinly sliced diagonally
2 spring onions, sliced diagonally
1 coriander sprig, leaves picked, to garnish

**FOR THE SWEET & SOUR SAUCE**
1 ripe pineapple, skin and core removed (you need about 525g/1lb 2½oz of fruit)
4 tablespoons vegetable oil
30g/1oz piece of root ginger, peeled and finely chopped
½ onion, finely chopped
200g/7oz palm sugar or light soft brown sugar
1 teaspoon salt
125g/4½oz tamarind concentrate or paste
4 teaspoons distilled white vinegar

1  First, make the sweet-and-sour sauce. Cut 125g/4½oz of the pineapple into 1cm/½in dice. Set aside the rest of the pineapple for the stir-fry. Heat the oil in a medium saucepan over a high heat. Add the pineapple, ginger and onion and fry for 2 minutes, stirring often, until softened. Add the sugar, salt, tamarind and vinegar, reduce the heat to medium and simmer for 10 minutes, stirring occasionally, until reduced and thickened. Remove and set aside.

2  Prepare the chicken. Mix together the plain flour, cornflour, salt and pepper in a large mixing bowl. Add the chicken and turn until coated in the seasoned flour mixture. Place the chicken in a sieve and shake off any excess flour.

3  Heat the oil in a large wok or deep-sided frying pan over a high heat and, when hot, add a third of the chicken and fry for 4 minutes, until crisp and golden. Using a slotted spoon, remove the chicken from the oil and drain on kitchen paper, while you repeat with the remaining chicken, adding more oil, if needed. Set aside all the fried chicken.

4  Cut the remaining pineapple into 3cm/1¼in cubes. Pour away all but 2 tablespoons of the oil from the wok or pan. Reheat the remaining oil over a high heat and add the pineapple cubes, onion, cherry tomatoes and both types of chilli and stir-fry for 3 minutes.

5  Stir in the fried chicken and the sweet-and-sour sauce. Turn until everything is combined and cook until the sauce is hot, about 3 minutes. Transfer the chicken and sauce to a serving platter, scatter over the spring onions and sprinkle with the coriander, then serve immediately.

# GINGER BEEF

**We have used beef in this recipe, but you could just as easily and deliciously substitute chicken, pork or seafood, if you prefer.**

**SERVES** 4
**PREP** 15 minutes, plus soaking
**COOK** 5 minutes

10g/¼oz dried wood ear
    mushrooms
2 tablespoons vegetable oil
400g/14oz beef tenderloin, trimmed
    and cut diagonally across the
    grain into 3mm/⅛in thick slices
100g/3½oz button mushrooms,
    cut in half
5 garlic cloves, finely chopped
50g/1¾oz piece of root ginger,
    peeled and thinly sliced
2 tablespoons soy bean paste
1 onion, thinly sliced
1 Thai red chilli, thinly sliced
    diagonally
1 Thai green chilli, thinly sliced
    diagonally
1 tablespoon oyster sauce
1 teaspoon caster sugar
2 spring onions, sliced diagonally

1  Put the wood ear mushrooms in a heatproof bowl and pour over just-boiled water from a kettle to cover. Leave the mushrooms to soften for 20 minutes. Drain well, discarding the soaking water, and set the mushrooms aside.

2  Heat a large wok or frying pan over a high heat. Add the oil and when very hot, add the beef and button mushrooms and stir-fry for 30 seconds, until the beef has browned. Add the garlic and stir-fry for 1 minute, then add the ginger and soy bean paste and cook for a further 30 seconds.

3  Finally, add the onion, both types of chilli and the hydrated wood ear mushrooms and stir-fry for a further 30 seconds. Add the oyster sauce and sugar, tossing the pan to combine, then add 4 tablespoons of water and the spring onions. Heat through for a minute or two, then transfer to a serving platter and serve immediately.

Wood ear mushrooms (or black fungi) are distinctively shaped – just like frilly ears. They grow on rotting bark in the humid forests of Southeast Asia and are used throughout Asian cooking. Although their own flavour is relatively mild, the mushrooms are wonderful for absorbing and displaying the flavours elsewhere in the dish.

gf 🌶

# PAD PED CHICKEN

**This is a drier version of a chicken stir-fry, flavoured with red curry paste. It's good to eat with jasmine, brown or sticky rice.**

**SERVES** 4
**PREP** 15 minutes
**COOK** 10 minutes

3 tablespoons vegetable oil
80g/2¾oz Red Curry Paste (see
    page 254) or ready-made paste
8 garlic cloves, finely chopped
400g/14oz boneless chicken thighs,
    each cut into 5–7 long slices
    (keep the fat on to add extra
    flavour)
2 tablespoons fish sauce
1 tablespoon palm sugar or light
    soft brown sugar
100g/3½oz green beans, cut in half
1 Thai red chilli, thinly sliced
    diagonally
8 kaffir lime leaves, finely shredded
8 Thai basil leaves or regular basil,
    to garnish

1  Heat 1 tablespoon of the oil in a small saucepan over a medium heat, add the red curry paste and fry for 2 minutes, stirring continuously, until you can smell the aroma of the paste. Remove and set aside.

2  Heat a large wok or frying pan over a high heat. Add the remaining oil and garlic and stir-fry for 1 minute. Next, add the chicken and stir-fry for 3 minutes.

3  Stir in the fish sauce, sugar, beans, chilli and 3 tablespoons of water and stir-fry for a further 2 minutes or until the chicken is cooked.

4  Finally, add the fried curry paste and the kaffir lime leaves. Stir well and cook for another 1–2 minutes to heat through. Transfer to a serving platter, scatter over the basil and serve immediately.

# SCALLOPS WITH COCONUT CHILLI DRESSING & CRISPY BASIL

Fresh scallops are so much better than frozen for this recipe. Frozen can remain watery, even if you drain and dry them well before searing, and it's difficult to get them to go a lovely golden colour. This is a treat of a dish and would work served as part of a large, special meal. The crispy basil leaves add a burst of flavour and texture – and look good, too.

**SERVES** 4
**PREP** 15 minutes
**COOK** 10 minutes

450g/1lb fresh scallops, about 16 in total
rapeseed oil, for frying
12 large Thai basil leaves or regular basil
Little Gem lettuce leaves, to serve
salt and freshly ground black pepper

**FOR THE COCONUT CHILLI DRESSING**
1 tablespoon cold-pressed rapeseed oil or olive oil
2 garlic cloves, finely chopped
1 medium-hot red chilli, deseeded and diced
juice of 1 lime
4 tablespoons coconut milk
a pinch of palm sugar or light soft brown sugar
1 tablespoon fish sauce

1  Trim the scallops and remove and reserve the corals if they have them. Rinse and pat dry thoroughly with paper towels, then season with salt and black pepper and set aside.

2  Put all the dressing ingredients in a small saucepan and warm them through for a couple of minutes, stirring occasionally.

3  Pour enough oil into a large wok or frying pan to generously coat the base. Add half of the basil leaves, spreading them out, and fry for 1 minute or until almost crisp. Leave them to drain on kitchen paper (they will crisp up further as they cool), then repeat with the remaining leaves. Set aside.

4  Pour off all but 1 tablespoon of the oil in the wok or pan and heat the remaining oil over a high heat. When the oil starts to smoke, place the prepared scallops in the wok or pan, making sure they do not touch each other – you may need to cook them in two batches if you can't spread them out enough. (If so, plate and serve the first batch while the second batch of scallops is cooking.) Sear the scallops for 1½–2 minutes on each side, depending on their size, until golden. A minute before the scallops are ready, add the corals to the pan and cook, turning once, until heated through. Take care not to overcook the scallops as you don't want them to turn rubbery. Meanwhile, reheat the sauce over a very low heat.

5  To serve, arrange the Little Gem leaves on a serving platter, top each leaf with 2–4 scallops (depending on their size) and spoon over a quarter of the sauce. Finally, scatter over the crispy basil leaves and serve immediately.

# WOK-SMOKED DUCK

**All you need is a large wok with a tight-fitting lid to smoke poultry, meat, seafood or vegetables – no specialist equipment or ingredients required! The smoking mixture in this recipe is a Thai-inspired combination of jasmine rice, cardamom, cloves and sugar, which when heated infuse the duck with a fragrant smokiness.**

**SERVES** 4
**PREP** 10 minutes
**COOK** 50 minutes

1 teaspoon 5-spice powder
1 teaspoon salt
3 tablespoons palm sugar or light
    soft brown sugar
4 duck breasts, skin on, excess
    fat trimmed
2 large handfuls jasmine rice
10 Thai cardamom or green
    cardamom pods, bruised
10 cloves
4 spring onions, thinly sliced
    diagonally, to serve
Sweet Chilli Sauce (see page 257)
    or sriracha sauce, to serve

**1** Mix together the 5-spice, salt and 1 tablespoon of the sugar in a bowl. Rub the mixture all over the duck breasts.

**2** Heat a large wok over a high heat. Place 2 duck breasts, skin-side down, in the wok and sear for 2 minutes or until evenly browned and crisp. Turn the duck over and sear the other side for 1 minute, until browned. Remove the duck from the wok and set aside while you brown the remaining duck.

**3** Wipe the wok clean and leave to cool slightly. When cool enough to handle, line the inside of the wok and lid with foil to protect them. Place the rice, cardamom, cloves and remaining sugar in the wok and stir until combined. Place a wok rack or pan stand on top so it sits above the smoking mixture in the base of the wok; make sure it's not touching.

**4** Heat the wok over a high heat and when the mixture starts to smoke, put the duck breasts on the rack and cover with the tight-fitting lid. Stuff any gaps between the wok base and lid with extra foil to stop any smoke escaping.

**5** Reduce the heat to medium–low, making sure the mixture in the wok is still smoking, and smoke the duck for 40 minutes. (You'll need to keep your kitchen well ventilated.) Turn off the heat and leave the duck to stand for 5 minutes.

**6** Remove the duck from the wok and thickly slice diagonally – the breasts should still be pink in the middle. Serve the duck sprinkled with the spring onions and with a spoonful of sweet chilli sauce or sriracha sauce on the side.

# CHICKEN STIR-FRY WITH BUTTERNUT SQUASH

**A traditional Thai–Chinese recipe, this dish is a favourite at parties and celebrations throughout Thailand. It's simple, warming and – as you'd expect – utterly irresistible.**

**SERVES** 4
**PREP** 15 minutes
**COOK** 10 minutes

2 tablespoons vegetable oil
4 boneless, skinless chicken
    breasts, cut into 3cm/1¼in cubes
1 onion, thinly sliced
200g/7oz steamed peeled butternut
    squash, cut into 2cm/¾in cubes

**FOR THE PASTE**
1 coriander stalk, roughly chopped
2 garlic cloves, roughly chopped
1cm/½in piece of root ginger,
    peeled and chopped
a pinch of ground white pepper
a pinch of salt

**FOR THE SAUCE**
a pinch of ground aniseed
a pinch of chilli powder
5 tablespoons sriracha sauce
½ tablespoon fish sauce
30g/1oz palm sugar or light soft
    brown sugar
1 tablespoon distilled white vinegar

**TO SERVE**
a handful roasted unsalted
    cashew nuts
3 whole dried chillies, toasted
    (see page 83)
1 spring onion, diagonally sliced

1  First, make the paste. Put all the paste ingredients in a pestle and mortar and pound until they are smooth. Alternatively, use a mini food processor or grinder. Set aside.

2  Next, make the sauce. Mix together all the sauce ingredients in a bowl, stirring until the sugar dissolves, then set aside.

3  To make the dish, heat a large wok or frying pan over a high heat. Add the vegetable oil and the prepared paste and stir-fry for 1 minute, until the paste smells aromatic.

4  Add the chicken and onion and stir-fry for 4–5 minutes, until the chicken is cooked through. Add the steamed squash, the prepared sauce and 200ml/7fl oz of water. Toss well until everything is combined and the chicken is coated in the sauce. Reduce the heat to medium and cook for 3 minutes, until the liquid has reduced and thickened.

5  Remove the pan from the heat and transfer the chicken mixture to a large serving bowl. Scatter over the cashews, crumble over the toasted dried chillies, and sprinkle over the spring onion, then serve immediately.

# TOFU & SPINACH STIR-FRY

**Tofu is wonderful at taking on the flavours of a stir-fry to make a meal to rival any meaty alternative. Here, the earthy soya bean sauce ensures a flavour-packed vegan dish.**

**SERVES** 4
**PREP** 20 minutes
**COOK** 20 minutes

70ml/2¼fl oz vegetable oil
400g/14oz firm tofu, drained well, patted dry and cut into 2cm/¾in cubes
150g/5½oz baby spinach leaves
1 Thai red chilli, thinly sliced diagonally
1 Thai green chilli, thinly sliced diagonally
1 tablespoon Golden Fried Shallots (see page 258) or ready-made crispy fried shallots, to serve (optional)

**FOR THE SOYA BEAN SAUCE**
30g/1oz peeled and finely grated root ginger
50g/1¾oz soy bean paste
30g/1oz yellow bean paste
1 tablespoon caster sugar
400g/14oz can soya beans, drained
1 teaspoon cornflour

1  First, make the soya bean sauce. Pour 500ml/17fl oz of water into a saucepan, add the ginger and bring to the boil. Reduce the heat, stir in the soy bean paste, yellow bean paste, sugar and soya beans and simmer for 10 minutes, stirring occasionally. Dissolve the cornflour in 1 tablespoon of water, pour it into the sauce and stir well until thickened slightly. Set aside.

2  Pour the oil into a large wok or frying pan and heat over a high heat. Add the tofu and fry, turning occasionally, for 5–8 minutes, until golden and crisp. Using a slotted spoon, remove the tofu and drain on kitchen paper. Set aside.

3  Reheat the sauce over a low heat. While it's reheating, pour all but 1 tablespoon of the oil out of the tofu wok or pan. Add the spinach and both types of chilli and stir-fry for 1 minute. Spoon the cooked spinach onto a serving platter and pile the tofu on top. Spoon the sauce over the top, then sprinkle with the golden fried shallots, if using. Serve immediately.

# CHAR-GRILL

The char-grill is one of our favourite pieces of cooking equipment in the Busaba restaurants, partly because it gives everything it cooks, from meat and poultry to seafood and vegetables, a great depth of flavour and rich slightly blackened colour. Our guests rave about our char-grilled calamari dish and its success is one of the reasons we buy tonnes and tonnes of squid every year!

In the street markets of Bangkok (and other parts of Thailand), peer through the aromatic smokiness and you'll see grills of various sizes char-grilling satays, pork, squid, prawns and chicken, among many other foods. It is one of the most popular ways to cook food on the street.

At home, the closest alternative to a char-grill is probably a charcoal barbecue. If the weather is kind (and even if it's not, but you're willing to brave it), barbecuing is suitable for every recipe in this chapter. Charcoal and lumpwood will provide you with the best smoky flavours, but gas or electric barbecues still have an air of authenticity about them.

However, we know that barbecuing isn't always the most accessible way to cook, so for ease we've given you methods that use a ridged griddle pan or regular grill. Whichever of these you use, preheat it first over a high heat to allow the food to cook quickly and achieve that seared, char-grilled flavour and aroma. Try to use the largest griddle pan you can find to allow the food to breathe and sear, rather than braise in its own juices. Also key is to oil the food, rather than the pan.

Whether you're char-grilling, griddling or grilling, remember that cooking times tend to be short: this is high-heat-for-quick-fix food. But, if you find your food burning, do turn down the heat a little – you don't want to end up with food that is black on the outside and raw in the middle, and that hasn't had the opportunity to gather that characteristic smokiness.

This chapter is full of wonderful marinades that add to the flavour of the food and, especially in the case of meat, help to tenderize it. Typical Thai marinades feature tamarind, rice vinegar, chilli, lime, spices, oyster sauce, soya-bean pastes, soy sauce, ginger and garlic. Palm sugar or honey gives food a deep, glossy colour and imparts a sweetness so characteristic of Thai cuisine – take care not to let it burn and turn bitter, though.

Another way to add flavour is to wrap food in banana leaves before char-grilling. This technique is perfect for containing delicate foods, such as fish, which may fall apart during cooking – and looks stunning when you bring it to the table.

# FRESHWATER PRAWNS WITH LIME DIPPING SAUCE

Wander through the plazas in Bangkok and see families tucking into the finger food that is prawns with lime dipping sauce. You can eat them just as they are, or as a light addition to a feast of grilled seafood.

**SERVES** 4
**PREP** 20 minutes, plus marinating
**COOK** 15 minutes

16 raw peeled freshwater or jumbo king prawns, deveined (defrosted if frozen)

**FOR THE MARINADE**
2 tablespoons flaked coconut
2 tablespoons Golden Fried Shallots (see page 258) or ready-made crispy fried shallots
125g/4½oz Red Curry Paste (see page 254) or ready-made paste
2 teaspoons ground turmeric
4 tablespoons vegetable oil
1 tablespoon tamarind concentrate or paste
a pinch of salt
1 tablespoon caster sugar

**FOR THE DIPPING SAUCE**
1 Thai red chilli, roughly chopped
1 Thai green chilli, roughly chopped
2 coriander sprigs, roughly chopped
4 garlic cloves, finely chopped
4 tablespoons fish sauce
100ml/3½fl oz lime juice
30g/1oz caster sugar

1  First, make the marinade. Mix together all the ingredients in a large mixing bowl. Add the prawns and turn them until coated all over. Cover and leave to marinate in the fridge for at least 2 hours, or preferably overnight.

2  Make the dipping sauce. Put both types of chilli, the coriander and the garlic in a large pestle and mortar and pound to form a fine paste. Alternatively, use a mini food processor or grinder. Scrape the paste into a bowl and stir in the fish sauce, lime juice and sugar until the sugar dissolves. Pour the dipping sauce into a serving bowl and set aside until the prawns are ready.

3  Heat a large ridged griddle pan or plate over a high heat. When hot, reduce the heat to medium and add the prawns (you may need to cook them in two batches) and cook for 6 minutes, turning once, until cooked. The prawns are white when ready.

4  To serve, arrange the prawns on a serving platter with the dipping sauce on the side.

> Dipping sauces are a way of life in Thai cooking. While we call them sauces, really they're more like condiments: flavour enhancers that make the best of every mouthful.

# GRILLED MACKEREL WITH CUCUMBER & CORIANDER RELISH

When buying oyster sauce – a thick, brown, flavourful condiment, traditionally made by slow-cooking oysters – look for one with the minimum number of additives and that actually includes oysters in the ingredients' list. A good-quality one will really make a difference to the taste of this dish and give a golden, slightly caramelized colour and umami (savoury) flavour to the mackerel. The zingy cucumber relish really cuts through the richness of the mackerel.

**SERVES** 4
**PREP** 15 minutes
**COOK** 10 minutes

4 tablespoons oyster sauce
1 teaspoon rapeseed oil
4 large or 8 small mackerel fillets, pin-boned
2 teaspoons toasted sesame seeds, to serve
lime wedges, to serve
salt and ground white pepper

**FOR THE CUCUMBER & CORIANDER RELISH**
2 teaspoons caster sugar
5 tablespoons rice vinegar
½ teaspoon salt
1 banana shallot, diced
1 medium-hot red chilli, deseeded and diced
½ cucumber, cut into ribbons using a vegetable peeler, seeds discarded
3 tablespoons chopped coriander leaves

1 First, start the cucumber and coriander relish. Pour 3 tablespoons of water into a small pan, stir in the sugar and warm over a medium heat for 1 minute. Add the vinegar and salt and heat for another 2 minutes, until it forms a light syrup. Remove from the heat and pour into a serving bowl. Stir in the shallot and leave to cool.

2 Meanwhile, preheat the grill to high and line the grill pan with foil. (Alternatively, cook the fish over a char-grill or in a griddle pan.) While the grill is heating, mix together the oyster sauce and oil and brush the mixture over both sides of each mackerel fillet. Season with salt and pepper.

3 Place the mackerel under the grill and grill for 3–4 minutes on each side, until golden.

4 Meanwhile, finish making the relish: simply stir the chilli, cucumber and coriander leaves into the cooled syrup.

5 Place equal amounts of the cucumber relish on individual plates, or on a serving platter. Top with the mackerel, then sprinkle the fish with the sesame seeds. Serve with wedges of lime by the side.

# 5-SPICE CHICKEN WITH PINEAPPLE & CHILLI RELISH

We all know that cooking over wood or charcoal gives a lovely smoky flavour, but you don't need to light a barbecue to achieve it at home, if you don't have time (or the weather isn't with you). You can achieve great flavour using a ridged griddle pan. It's important to let the chicken marinate in the spices for at least an hour or preferably overnight. The fruity relish delivers a chilli hit with good poke that goes really well with the chicken. Serve the recipe with sticky rice, if you wish.

**SERVES** 4
**PREP** 15 minutes, plus marinating
**COOK** 10 minutes

4 boneless, skinless chicken
    breasts
1 teaspoon 5-spice powder
1 tablespoon sriracha sauce
1 tablespoon rapeseed oil
juice of 1 lime
1 teaspoon light soy sauce
salt and ground white pepper

**FOR THE PINEAPPLE & CHILLI RELISH**
2 tablespoons fish sauce
1 teaspoon palm sugar or light soft
    brown sugar
1 banana shallot, finely chopped
1 medium-hot red chilli, deseeded
    and diced
1 small ripe pineapple, skin and
    core removed, diced
a handful Thai basil leaves or
    regular basil, torn

1 Put the chicken breasts between two large sheets of cling film and bash with a meat mallet or the end of a rolling pin until evenly flattened and about 1cm/½in thick.

2 Mix together the 5-spice, sriracha sauce, oil, lime juice and soy sauce in a large non-reactive shallow dish. Season with salt and pepper, add the chicken and spoon the marinade over until the meat is evenly coated. Cover and marinate in the fridge for at least 1 hour or preferably overnight.

3 To make the relish, mix together the fish sauce and sugar in a medium serving bowl until the sugar dissolves. Add the rest of the ingredients, apart from the basil, and set aside.

4 Heat a large ridged griddle pan over a high heat. When hot, turn the heat down slightly and add the chicken (you may need to cook it in two batches) and cook for 5–8 minutes, turning once, until golden and cooked through with no trace of pink in the middle.

5 Finish off the relish by stirring in the basil, then serve the chicken on individual plates with a good spoonful of relish by the side.

# TAMARIND DUCK

If you put duck on a Thai menu, you know it's a special occasion. From New Year festivities to wedding parties, duck is a sign of celebration. Here, we're using duck breasts, but in Thailand the duck is often cooked and served whole.

**SERVES** 4
**PREP** 20 minutes, plus marinating
**COOK** 30 minutes

4 large duck breasts, skin on,
    fat trimmed
3 tablespoons vegetable oil
200g/7oz Chinese broccoli (gai lan
    or kailan), sliced diagonally into
    4cm/1½in lengths
4 coriander leaves, to garnish
½ thinly sliced Thai red chilli,
    to garnish

**FOR THE MARINADE**
4 tablespoons oyster sauce
a pinch of ground white pepper
3 tablespoons light soy sauce
1 tablespoon dark soy sauce
1 teaspoon caster sugar
20g/¾oz coriander leaves,
    finely chopped
2 tablespoons clear honey

**FOR THE TAMARIND SAUCE**
250g/9oz tamarind concentrate
    or paste
150g/5½oz palm sugar or light soft
    brown sugar
a pinch of salt
1 tablespoon distilled white vinegar
a pinch of dried chilli flakes

1  First, make the marinade. Mix together all the ingredients in a large shallow dish until the sugar dissolves. Next, add the duck breasts and turn them until coated all over. Cover and leave to marinate in the fridge overnight.

2  To make the tamarind sauce, put all the ingredients, except the chilli flakes, in a medium saucepan with 455ml/16fl oz of water. Bring to the boil, then reduce the heat to low and simmer for 20 minutes, until reduced and thickened. Stir in the chilli flakes and set aside.

3  Remove the duck breasts from the marinade (discard the marinade). Heat a large ridged griddle pan or grill plate over a high heat. When hot, turn the heat down to medium and add the duck breasts, skin-side down, and griddle for 5 minutes, until golden. Turn the breasts over and cook for a further 3 minutes, until browned on the outside, but still pink in the middle. (You may need to cook the duck in two batches.) Remove from the pan, cover and leave to rest for 5 minutes.

4  While the duck is resting, heat a large wok or frying pan over a high heat. Add the oil and when hot, stir-fry the broccoli for 2 minutes, until just tender. Arrange the broccoli on a large serving platter. Slice the duck breasts at an angle and arrange on top of the broccoli.

5  Meanwhile, reheat the tamarind sauce for 2 minutes. When the sauce reaches the boil, remove it from the heat and spoon it over the duck. Serve garnished with the coriander leaves and red chilli.

# RED CURRY BURGER WITH THAI SLAW

**The classic Thai red curry paste is much more versatile than you may think. It's well worth making a batch to use in curries, dressings, sauces and, of course, to flavour this Thai-inspired beef burger.**

**SERVES** 4
**PREP** 30 minutes, plus chilling
**COOK** 10 minutes

500g/1lb 2oz beef mince, about 30% fat content
2 large garlic cloves, minced
4cm/1½in piece of root ginger, peeled and finely chopped
4 teaspoons Red Curry Paste (see page 254) or ready-made paste
1 banana shallot, finely diced
a handful coriander leaves, chopped
1 egg, lightly beaten
rapeseed oil, for brushing
4 brioche buns, split; crisp lettuce leaves; and sliced pickled or fresh cucumber, to serve
salt and freshly ground black pepper

**FOR THE THAI SLAW**
juice of 1 lime
2 teaspoons fish sauce
1 teaspoon caster sugar
1 teaspoon rice vinegar
125g/4½oz white cabbage, shredded
3 carrots, coarsely grated
1 tablespoon chopped mint leaves
2 tablespoons chopped coriander leaves
1 teaspoon black sesame seeds

**FOR THE SWEET CHILLI MAYO**
4 tablespoons mayonnaise
1 tablespoon Sweet Chilli Sauce (see page 257) or sriracha sauce
juice of 1 lime

1  In a large mixing bowl, mix together the mince, garlic, ginger, red curry paste, shallot and coriander. Season with salt and pepper and stir in the egg until combined. Form the mixture into 4 large burgers and chill, covered, for 30 minutes to firm up.

2  While the burgers are chilling, make the Thai slaw. Mix together the lime juice, fish sauce, sugar and rice vinegar in a large serving bowl. Season with salt and pepper. Add the cabbage, carrots and herbs, then turn until everything is combined. Scatter the sesame seeds over the top and set aside. The slaw is best served at room temperature.

3  Mix together all the ingredients for the sweet chilli mayo and set aside.

4  Heat a large ridged griddle pan over a high heat (or you can use a char-grill or barbecue). Brush both sides of each burger with oil and place in the pan. Turn the heat down slightly and griddle for 4–5 minutes on each side, until golden on the outside and juicy and slightly pink in the middle. Leave to rest, covered, for 5 minutes while you toast the brioche buns in the griddle pan.

5  To serve, place a salad leaf and a few pickled or fresh cucumber slices on one half of each bun. Top with the burger and a good spoonful of the sweet chilli mayo. Top with the second half of bun and serve with the Thai slaw by the side.

# SEA BREAM PARCELS

For a truly local Thai cooking experience, you'd make this dish by covering the fish in wet clay and baking it on an outdoor char-grill (take a look at the panel, below). But, on a regular day, you can wrap the fish in foil and use a griddle.

**SERVES** 4
**PREP** 20 minutes
**COOK** 15–30 minutes, depending on the size of your griddle

100g/3½oz Red Curry Paste (see page 254) or ready-made paste
4 whole sea bream, scaled, gutted and cleaned
banana leaves, for wrapping
a large handful Thai basil leaves or regular basil
sea salt

**FOR THE DRESSING**
5 Thai red chillies
5 Thai green chillies
6 garlic cloves
juice of 1 lime
2 teaspoons caster sugar
4 tablespoons fish sauce
3 coriander sprigs

1  First, make the dressing. Put all the ingredients in a mini food processor or blender and blitz until roughly chopped; do not blend too finely. Spoon the dressing into a serving bowl and set aside.

2  Rub 2 tablespoons of red curry paste over both sides of each sea bream.

3  Place a piece of foil large enough to wrap one of the bream on a baking tray, then lay a banana leaf on top. Place one of the bream in the middle of the banana leaf and fill the belly cavity with Thai basil leaves and season with salt. Wrap the banana leaf around the bream, then wrap the foil over and tuck in the ends to secure. Repeat with each bream.

4  Heat a large ridged griddle pan over a high heat (or you can use a char-grill or barbecue). When hot, turn the heat down slightly and griddle the bream parcels for 8–10 minutes on one side, then turn and cook for a further 4–5 minutes, until the fish is cooked. (You may need to cook the bream in two batches.) Alternatively, bake in an oven preheated to 200°C/400°F/Gas 6 for 10 minutes.

5  Place a parcel on each serving plate and let everyone open their own to enjoy the aroma. Serve the dressing on the side.

If you want to have a go at cooking the fish in clay, any clay will do – even the kind you buy in your local art store. Completely wrap the fish in banana leaves, then mould the clay around the parcel. Place the parcel directly on the white-hot charcoals of a barbecue and cook for 10 minutes on each side. Remove the fish from the coals and carefully crack open the clay. Transfer to a plate and allow your guests to open their parcel themselves.

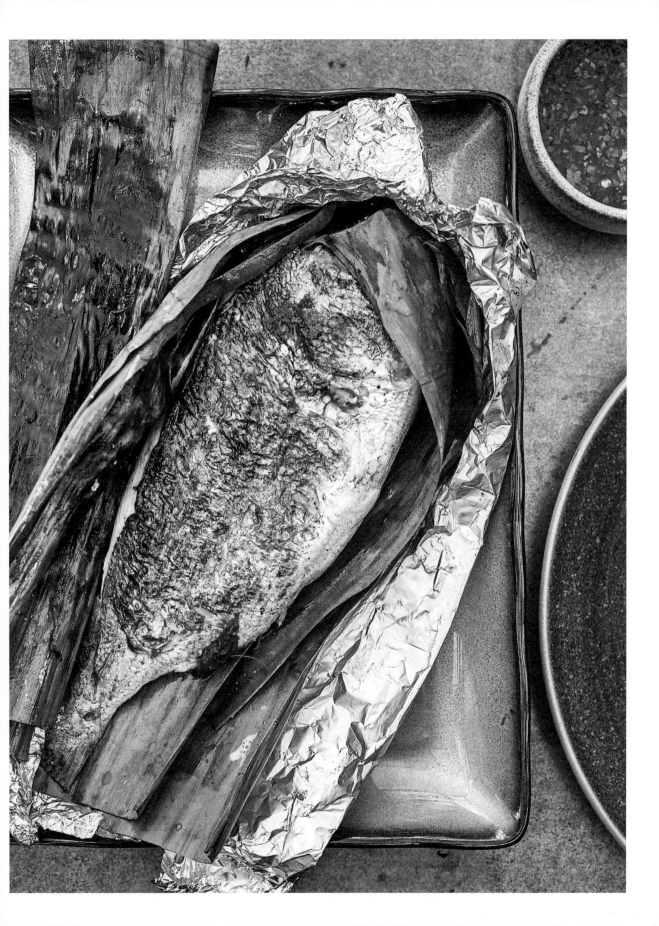

# CLASSIC THAI BEEF

Also known as 'Weeping Tiger', this famous recipe originates from the northeast of Thailand, at the border with Laos. The name 'Weeping Tiger' has unclear origins – some say that the marks on good beef reminded cooks of tiger stripes; others that the good meat is used for the dish, leaving the disconsolate tiger with nothing to eat but the chewy bits.

**SERVES** 4
**PREP** 15 minutes, plus marinating
**COOK** 15 minutes

4 tablespoons caster sugar
125ml/4fl oz light soy sauce
4 ribeye steaks, about 150g/5½oz each
micro mint leaves and crushed toasted rice, to garnish (optional)
salt and ground white pepper

**FOR THE DIPPING SAUCE**
200ml/7fl oz tamarind concentrate or paste
50g/1¾oz palm sugar or light soft brown sugar
100ml/3½fl oz fish sauce
1 teaspoon dried chilli flakes
1 banana shallot, thinly sliced
2 coriander sprigs, finely chopped
1 tablespoon finely chopped spring onion
10 mint leaves, finely shredded
½ lime
1 tablespoon uncooked jasmine or sticky rice, toasted and ground (see page 100)

1 To make a marinade for the beef, put the caster sugar and 1 teaspoon of water in a small saucepan, swirl the pan and warm over a medium heat, without stirring, until the sugar caramelizes and turns a dark brown. Remove from heat and stir in the light soy sauce. Set aside to cool.

2 Put the steaks in a large shallow dish, pour over the marinade and turn until coated all over. Cover and leave to marinate in the fridge for 1 hour.

3 Next, make the dipping sauce. Put the tamarind, sugar, fish sauce and chilli flakes in a mixing bowl and stir until the sugar dissolves. Pour the mixture into a serving bowl and stir in the shallot, coriander, spring onion and mint. Add the lime juice and stir in the toasted ground rice, then set aside.

4 Season the steaks with salt and white pepper. Heat a large ridged griddle pan over a high heat (or you can use a char-grill or barbecue). When hot, place the steaks in the pan and griddle for 3 minutes on one side, then turn over and cook for another 2 minutes for medium-cooked. (You will probably need to cook the steaks in two batches.) Remove from the pan and leave to rest for 5 minutes.

5 Cut the steaks into 2cm/¾in thick slices and arrange on a serving platter, then sprinkle with the micro mint leaves and ground toasted rice. Serve with the dipping sauce on the side. (The Som Tam Salad on page 202 makes a delicious accompaniment.)

# DUCK & CHICKEN BURGER WITH MANGO RELISH

**The Thais regard burgers and hotdogs as snack food. Popping up on menus and at street-food stalls all over Bangkok, burgers are definitely the dish that most obviously shouts Asian with a Western influence.**

**SERVES** 4
**PREP** 20 minutes, plus chilling
**COOK** 10 minutes

2 skin-on duck breasts
400g/14oz boneless, skinless
    chicken thighs
1 Thai red chilli, finely chopped
2 spring onions, finely chopped
2 garlic cloves, finely chopped
1 teaspoon salt
a large pinch of ground black
    pepper
1 tablespoon vegetable oil
4 sesame seed burger buns, split;
    crisp lettuce leaves; sliced
    tomato and cucumber; and
    Sweet Chilli Sauce (see page
    257) or sriracha sauce, to serve

**FOR THE MANGO RELISH**
1 small ripe mango, peeled, stoned
    and cut into small dice
1 Thai red chilli, deseeded and
    finely chopped
1 spring onion, finely chopped
a handful Thai basil leaves or
    regular basil, chopped
1 teaspoon fish sauce
juice of ½ lime

1  Put the duck and chicken into a food processor and process until coarsely minced. Transfer the mince to a large mixing bowl with the chilli, spring onions, garlic, salt and pepper and mix well, massaging the mixture with your hands, until combined. Form the mixture into 4 equally sized balls, then flatten and press each ball into a round patty, about 2cm/¾in thick. Cover and chill for 30 minutes to firm up.

2  While the burgers are chilling, make the mango relish simply by mixing together all the ingredients in a bowl. Set aside.

3  Heat a large ridged griddle pan over a high heat (or you can use a char-grill or barbecue). Brush both sides of each burger with oil and place them in the pan. Turn the heat down slightly and griddle for 2–3 minutes on each side or until golden and cooked through – there should be no trace of pink in the middle. Leave to rest, covered, while you toast the burger buns in the griddle pan.

4  To serve, spread some sweet chilli sauce or sriracha sauce on the base of each bun, top with a lettuce leaf, a burger, tomato and cucumber slices, and then a spoonful of the mango relish. Finish off with the second half of the bun and serve straightaway.

# STEAM & BRAISE

In this chapter, traditional Thai meets world fusion, with a collection of dishes and flavours that really tap into the cross-cultural vibe of modern Bangkok Thai. Despite the modern feel of these recipes, steaming and braising are two classic Thai methods of cooking. If you're adopting a Western way of eating, with dishes served as separate courses rather than as a single feast, each of these recipes is perfect as a main meal served with a side dish or two (see pages 190–205).

Steaming, usually in a bamboo basket, is perfect for mild-tasting ingredients such as dumplings, fish, shellfish, chicken, savoury and sweet egg custards, and vegetables. Traditional Thai chefs like to wrap food, particularly whole fish, in banana leaves before steaming; the leaves not only look pleasing, they also protect the delicate ingredients while cooking and infuse them with flavour. Steaming is healthy, too, retaining nutrients that might otherwise be lost during the heating process.

If you're lucky enough to have more than one bamboo steaming basket, stack them on top of one another to cook multiple portions or multiple dishes at once. Just be aware that the flavours can seep into one another, so avoid cooking anything too strongly flavoured at the same time as a mild-tasting food. It's important not to over-fill the steaming basket, otherwise the steam won't be able to penetrate the food or cook it evenly; and during cooking do keep an eye on the water level underneath the basket, as you don't want it to run dry.

If you don't have a bamboo steamer, you don't need to rush out and buy one. A stainless steel steamer is a perfectly good alternative, even if it doesn't look quite as authentic!

Unlike steaming, which tends to be a quick method of cooking, braising (or pot-roasting) is slow and contemplative and works well with cheaper cuts of meat and poultry, tenderizing them as they release their otherwise locked-in aromas. The start of the braising process is searing or browning over a high heat. Don't be tempted to skip this step as it adds not only colour, but flavour, too. Once you're done with the browning, sit back and leave the dishes to braise to their best – you'll be rewarded with richly flavoured food with the minimum of effort.

# SLOW-COOKED SPICED PORK BELLY

**This is a rich and hearty Thai stew. The pork belly is infused with an aromatic mix of star anise, fennel seeds, chilli, garlic, ginger and soy sauce. Serve the dish simply with jasmine rice.**

**SERVES** 4
**PREP** 20 minutes
**COOK** 1 hour 50 minutes

1 tablespoon vegetable oil, plus extra if needed
1kg/2lb 4oz pork belly slices, skin removed, each slice cut into 3 pieces
3 banana shallots, sliced
1 teaspoon fennel seeds
1 tablespoon light soy sauce
2 tablespoons dark soy sauce
1 tablespoon fish sauce
1 tablespoon rice vinegar
1 teaspoon palm sugar or light soft brown sugar
2 star anise
2 spring onions, sliced, to serve
coriander leaves, to serve

**FOR THE PASTE**
5 garlic cloves, roughly chopped
5cm/2in piece of root ginger, peeled and roughly chopped
1 Thai red chilli, deseeded and chopped
1 banana shallot, roughly chopped
3 tablespoons chopped coriander stalks

1  Put all the ingredients for the paste in a mini food processor with a splash of water and blitz to a paste. Set aside.

2  Heat the oil in a large heavy-based saucepan over a high heat and brown the pork belly pieces in three batches, adding extra oil if needed. It will take about 5 minutes per batch. Remove the pork from the pan and set aside.

3  Reduce the heat to medium, add the prepared paste, along with the shallots and fennel seeds to the pan and cook for 2 minutes, stirring. Return the pork belly and add the light and dark soy sauces, and the fish sauce, rice vinegar, sugar and star anise. Pour in 400ml/14fl oz of water and stir until combined, then bring to the boil.

4  Reduce the heat to low, cover and simmer for 1½ hours or until the pork is tender. Add extra water during the cooking time to keep the pork moist, if needed.

5  Serve the pork with the cooking juices spooned over the top, and sprinkled with spring onions and coriander leaves.

# POACHED CHICKEN IN COCONUT WITH THAI PESTO

This light, summery dish captures the classic flavours of Thai cooking, but with a modern twist. You could make the coconut broth a day in advance and simply reheat it when you're ready to cook the chicken. Similarly, the Thai pesto will keep for up to three days in an airtight container in the fridge.

**SERVES** 4
**PREP** 20 minutes
**COOK** 20 minutes

3 banana shallots, roughly chopped
2 lemongrass sticks, peeled and roughly chopped
2 large garlic cloves, roughly chopped
4cm/1½in piece of root ginger, peeled and roughly chopped
1 tablespoon cold-pressed rapeseed oil
400ml/14fl oz can coconut milk
200ml/7fl oz chicken stock
1 medium-hot red chilli, deseeded and thinly sliced into rings
1 tablespoon fish sauce
1 teaspoon palm sugar or light soft brown sugar
4 kaffir lime leaves
4 boneless, skinless chicken breasts, sliced lengthways into 2.5cm/1in wide strips
125g/4½oz asparagus tips
100g/3½oz sugar snap peas
lime wedges, to serve (optional)

**FOR THE THAI PESTO**
40g/1½oz unsalted cashew nuts
40g/1½oz pine nuts
25g/1oz Thai basil sprigs or regular basil, plus extra to garnish
10g/¼oz mint leaves
4 teaspoons fish sauce
2 garlic cloves, roughly chopped
1 medium-hot red chilli, deseeded and diced
125ml/4fl oz cold-pressed rapeseed oil
salt and ground white pepper

1  Put the shallots, lemongrass, garlic and ginger in a mini food processor and blitz to a paste.

2  Heat the oil in a large heavy-based saucepan over a medium–high heat. Add the paste and cook, stirring, for 2 minutes, until it smells aromatic. Stir in the coconut milk, stock, chilli, fish sauce, sugar and kaffir lime leaves and bring to the boil. Turn down the heat to low and simmer for 10 minutes, covered, to let the aromatics infuse the sauce.

3  Meanwhile, make the pesto. Grind the cashews and pine nuts in a mini food processor, then tip them into a mixing bowl. Add the basil, mint, fish sauce and garlic to the processor and blitz to a paste. Stir the paste into the nuts with the chilli and oil. Season with salt and pepper to taste, then set aside.

4  Continue to make the coconut broth. Increase the heat to medium, stir in the chicken and cook for 5 minutes. Add the asparagus and sugar snaps and cook for another 3 minutes, until the chicken is cooked through and the vegetables are just tender.

5  Using a slotted spoon, divide the chicken and vegetables between four warmed large serving bowls and ladle the coconut broth over the top. Top with a spoonful of pesto and a few extra basil leaves, and lime wedges on the side for squeezing over, if you like. (You may have some pesto left over: transfer it to a lidded container and keep it in the fridge for up to three days.)

# TAMARIND BEEF & SWEET POTATO

**In this recipe, the beef is slow-cooked in a rich spicy gravy until melt-in-the-mouth tender, while the sweet potato adds a burst of colour. Tamarind, a pod-like fruit with a sweet–sour taste and dark, sticky texture, comes in many forms. You can buy it still in the pod, in a firm block or in concentrate or paste form. When buying a paste, look for a brand with the minimum number of additives for a pure, intense flavour.**

**SERVES** 4
**PREP** 15 minutes
**COOK** 1 hour 50 minutes

2 onions, roughly chopped
3 large garlic cloves
5cm/2in piece of root ginger, peeled
and thinly sliced
1 large handful coriander sprigs,
stalks and leaves separated
2 tablespoons rapeseed oil
650g/1lb 7oz diced beef brisket or
chuck steak, trimmed of excess
fat
400ml/14fl oz can coconut milk
455ml/16fl oz beef stock
2 tablespoons tamarind
concentrate or paste
6 Thai cardamom or green
cardamom pods, bruised
1 small cinnamon stick
2 Thai red chillies, deseeded
and thinly sliced
4 kaffir lime leaves
750g/1lb 10oz sweet potatoes,
peeled and cut into large
bite-sized pieces
salt and freshly ground black
pepper

1 Put the onions, garlic, ginger and coriander stalks in a mini food processor and blitz to a paste.

2 Heat the oil in a large heavy-based saucepan over a high heat. Add the beef and fry for 5 minutes, until browned all over. (You may need to do this in two batches.) Remove the beef and set aside.

3 Reduce the heat to medium, add the onion paste and cook, stirring, for 2 minutes, until it smells aromatic. Return the beef to the pan and turn until coated in the paste.

4 Pour in the coconut milk and stock, then stir in the tamarind, cardamom, cinnamon, half the chilli slices, and the kaffir lime leaves and bring to the boil. Reduce the heat to low, cover, and simmer for 1 hour.

5 Add the sweet potatoes and cook for another 30 minutes or until the beef is tender and the sauce has reduced and thickened. Stir occasionally and add a splash of water if the sauce becomes too thick or leave the lid off if there is too much liquid.

6 Season with salt and pepper, to taste, and serve with the remaining chilli and the coriander leaves scattered over the top, if you wish.

# MUSHROOM LARB CABBAGE WRAPS WITH BROTH

A variation on the classic northern Thai hot-and-sour salad, this mushroom larb is inspired by the increasingly popular fusion-food scene in Bangkok. The larb is steamed in a cabbage-leaf wrap and comes with an aromatic mushroom broth, which can be either poured over the wrap or served in a small cup by the side.

**SERVES** 4
**PREP** 20 minutes, plus soaking
**COOK** 30 minutes

2 tablespoons jasmine rice
3 tablespoons groundnut oil
3 large garlic cloves, finely chopped
5cm/2in piece of root ginger, peeled and finely chopped
480g/1lb 1oz chestnut mushrooms, roughly chopped
1 large lemongrass stick, peeled and finely chopped
1 Thai red chilli, deseeded and finely chopped
3 kaffir lime leaves, shredded
3 tablespoons tamarind concentrate or paste
1 teaspoon palm sugar or light soft brown sugar
6 spring onions, finely chopped
juice of ½ lime
8 large round cabbage leaves
a handful coriander leaves, chopped, to serve
salt and freshly ground black pepper

**FOR THE MUSHROOM BROTH**
55g/2oz dried shiitake mushrooms
2 tablespoons light soy sauce
2 kaffir lime leaves
2.5cm/1in piece of root ginger, peeled and sliced into matchsticks

1  First, make the mushroom broth. Put the dried shiitake mushrooms in a heatproof mixing bowl and pour over 500ml/17fl oz of just-boiled water from a kettle. Cover and leave to soak for 1 hour or until softened. Strain, reserving the soaking liquid. Finely chop the rehydrated mushrooms, discarding any tough stalks, and set aside. Put the reserved soaking liquid in a small pan with the soy sauce, kaffir lime leaves and ginger. Bring to the boil, then reduce the heat to low and simmer, covered, for 5 minutes. Turn off the heat and set aside to let the aromatics flavour the broth.

2  Meanwhile, toast the rice in a large dry wok or frying pan, tossing the pan, until light golden all over, about 2–3 minutes. Tip the rice into a pestle and mortar and grind to a fine powder. Set aside and leave to cool.

3  Heat the groundnut oil in the wok or pan over a high heat, add the garlic, ginger, fresh and rehydrated mushrooms and stir-fry for 10 minutes or until softened. Add the lemongrass, chilli, kaffir lime leaves, tamarind and sugar, stir until combined, then warm through. Turn off the heat, stir in the spring onions and lime juice and season with salt and pepper, to taste.

4  To make the cabbage leaves easier to fold, make a v-shaped cut in the centre of each leaf to remove the tough part of the stalk. Divide the mushroom mixture between the 8 leaves. Taking one of the leaves, fold in the ends, then fold over the sides in the same way you would make a spring roll. Secure with wooden cocktail sticks. Repeat with all the cabbage leaves and mushroom filling to make eight parcels in total.

5  Steam the cabbage leaves in a tiered basket over a wok or pan of simmering water for 8 minutes or until the cabbage leaves are tender. (You may need to cook them in two batches.) At the same time, reheat the broth. To serve, open each parcel slightly and pour over a little of the broth (you can serve any remaining broth in small cups by the side). Scatter over the coriander before serving.

# JASMINE RIBS

**Braising these ribs slowly with the jasmine tea, spices, plum sauce and ginger cooks the meat until mouth-wateringly tender, as well as infusing it with flavour. The finale, roasting the ribs in a hot oven (or, cooking them on a barbecue, outdoor char-grill or indoor grill pan, if you prefer) gives them a golden, sticky coating.**

**SERVES** 4
**PREP** 20 minutes
**COOK** 3 hours 30 minutes

2 tablespoons vegetable oil, plus extra if needed
4 x 250g/9oz single beef short ribs, about 20cm/8in long
75g/2½oz piece of root ginger, sliced into rounds
100g/3½oz plum sauce
1 tablespoon black cardamom pods, bruised
235g/8½oz tomato ketchup
115ml/3¾fl oz distilled white vinegar
270g/9½oz palm sugar or light soft brown sugar
1 tablespoon loose jasmine leaf tea
1 tablespoon salt

**FOR THE SPICY CUCUMBER SALAD**
2 tablespoons fish sauce
1 tablespoon tamarind concentrate or paste
4 garlic cloves, finely sliced
finely grated zest and juice of 1 lime
2 Thai red chillies, thinly sliced
1 Thai green chilli, thinly sliced
2 coriander sprigs, finely chopped
8 cherry tomatoes, cut in half
1 cucumber, thinly sliced

**TO SERVE**
1 spring onion, finely sliced
2 tablespoons finely chopped roasted and unsalted peanuts
1 teaspoon Golden Fried Garlic (see page 258) or ready-made crispy fried shallots (optional)

1  Heat the oil in a large heavy-based saucepan over a high heat. Add half of the ribs and cook for about 5 minutes, until browned and sealed on both sides. Remove from the pan and brown the remaining ribs, adding more oil if needed. Set aside.

2  Return the ribs to the pan and add the ginger, plum sauce, cardamom, tomato ketchup, vinegar, sugar, jasmine tea, and salt. Pour in 2 litres/70fl oz of water and bring to the boil. Reduce the heat, cover with a lid and simmer for 2½ hours, until the meat is tender. Remove the beef ribs from the pan and set aside.

3  Continue to cook the sauce in the pan, leaving the lid off, for 30–45 minutes, until the liquid has reduced and thickened to a ketchup consistency. Set aside.

4  While the sauce is cooking, make the spicy cucumber salad. Put the fish sauce, tamarind concentrate or paste, garlic and lime zest and juice in a small bowl and combine to make a dressing. Put the remaining ingredients in a large bowl and toss gently to combine, then pour over the dressing. Mix well to combine and set aside. (Alternatively, you can put the chillies and garlic in a large pestle and mortar and pound to a coarse paste. Add the coriander, tomatoes and cucumber and gently pound until crushed to the consistency of a chunky guacamole, then stir in the fish sauce, tamarind, lime zest and juice.)

5  Preheat the oven to 200°C/400°F/Gas 6. When the sauce is ready, put the ribs on a large baking tray and generously brush the sauce over both sides of each. Roast for 10 minutes, turning once and occasionally basting with the sauce until it forms a good glossy glaze.

6  Place the ribs on a large serving platter. Scatter over the spring onion, peanuts and fried garlic, if using, and serve with the spicy cucumber salad and bowls of jasmine rice.

# SEAFOOD CURRY IN BANANA BASKETS

Banana leaves are used in Thai cooking for both wrapping and presenting food, but their use is not simply visual as the leaves also add aroma and flavour. Find the leaves online or in Asian grocers, usually in the freezer or chiller sections. If frozen, allow the leaves to defrost before use – they don't take long. Here, the banana leaves are turned into small baskets, which hold the thick seafood curry. If you can't find banana leaves, cook the seafood curry in ramekins in a water bath. Once cooked, the curry sets into a type of savoury custard.

**SERVES** 4
**PREP** 25 minutes
**COOK** 15 minutes

2 large banana leaves, defrosted if frozen
160g/5¾oz can coconut cream (not the hard block known as creamed coconut)
1–2 tablespoons Red Curry Paste (see page 254) or ready-made paste
1 tablespoon fish sauce
juice of 1 lime, plus lime wedges, to serve
1 egg, lightly beaten
15g/½oz rice flour
4 kaffir lime leaves, finely shredded
450g/1lb skinless salmon fillet, cut into bite-sized pieces
100g/3½oz raw king or tiger prawns, deveined and cut into bite-sized pieces
75g/2½oz white cabbage, shredded
1 medium-hot red chilli, deseeded and thinly sliced, to serve
a handful basil leaves, torn, to serve
salt and ground white pepper

1 Rinse the banana leaves well before use. If the leaves are very firm, soak them in boiling water until softened. Measure 4 x 18cm/7in squares, avoiding the leaves' central spine, and cut out the squares with a pair of scissors. Take one of the squares and make a 6cm/2½in diagonal cut inwards from each corner, then overlap the corners and staple to secure the sides and make a basket shape. You could alternatively secure the corners with wooden cocktail sticks or tie a piece of string around the basket. Repeat to make four baskets in total. Cut 4 x 10cm/4in squares from the remaining leaves and use these to line the base of each basket to strengthen.

2 Mix together the coconut cream, 1 tablespoon of the red curry paste, the fish sauce and the lime juice. Taste the mixture and add the remaining paste, if needed, then the egg, rice flour and half the kaffir lime leaves. Stir until combined, season with salt and pepper, then fold in the salmon and prawns.

3 Divide the cabbage leaves between each basket, then spoon the seafood mixture on top. Put the filled banana-leaf baskets in a tiered steamer basket in a wok or pan. Cover and steam over simmering water for about 12–15 minutes, until the fish is cooked and the sauce sets like a savoury custard. (Alternatively, spoon the cabbage and fish mixture into four large ramekins, place in a sauté pan and pour in enough just-boiled water to come halfway up the sides of the ramekins. Allow the water to simmer over a low heat for 12–15 minutes to cook the curry as above.)

4 Just before serving, sprinkle the remaining lime leaves, along with the chilli slices and torn basil over the top of each basket.

# STEAMED STUFFED CRAB

**You need four ready-dressed crabs in their shells for this light dish, which is equally wonderful served as a starter or as part of a larger multi-dish meal. It is very easy to make and impressive to look at – the crabmeat is simply mixed with prawns, lemongrass, ginger and garlic and then stuffed back into the shell before steaming. Serve the crabs with the chilli-lime sauce and crisp lettuce leaves on the side.**

**SERVES** 4
**PREP** 20 minutes
**COOK** 15 minutes

4 small dressed crabs, about
    300g/10½oz crabmeat in total
175g/6oz raw peeled king or tiger
    prawns, deveined and roughly
    chopped
1 large lemongrass stick, peeled
    and finely chopped
2 large garlic cloves, crushed
4cm/1½in piece of root ginger,
    peeled and finely chopped
1 medium-hot red chilli, deseeded
    and finely chopped
3 spring onions, finely chopped
2 tablespoons chopped coriander
    leaves
1 tablespoon rapeseed oil
1 egg, separated
Little Gem lettuce leaves, to serve
salt and ground white pepper

**FOR THE CHILLI-LIME SAUCE**
1 medium-hot red chilli, deseeded
    and finely chopped
juice of 1 lime
1 tablespoon rice vinegar
1 teaspoon caster sugar
5cm/2in piece of cucumber,
    quartered lengthways, deseeded
    and diced

1  Scoop the crabmeat out of the crab shells into a mixing bowl, then stir in the prawns, lemongrass, garlic, ginger, chilli, spring onions, coriander and oil. Season with salt and pepper.

2  Beat the egg white lightly, then stir it into the crab mixture until combined. This will help to bind the filling when steamed. Spoon the filling back into the crab shells and brush the egg yolk over the tops to seal.

3  Place the crab shells in a tiered steamer basket, or on a trivet, placed over a wok or pan of simmering water. Cover and steam for 12–15 minutes, until the stuffing firms up and is cooked through. (For a more golden top, flash the crabs briefly under a hot grill.)

4  While the crab is steaming, mix together the ingredients for the chilli-lime sauce with 1 tablespoon of warm water until combined.

5  Place the crab shells on four individual plates or on a serving platter with some lettuce leaves on the side. Spoon the chilli-lime sauce over the top just before serving, or serve in a bowl for your guests to sprinkle over, to taste.

# THAI SALADS & VEGETABLE SIDES

Thai salads (or *yam*, meaning tossed or mixed together) are usually more than just a side dish, snack or appetizer. Many make a filling main meal with the addition of cooked noodles, meat, poultry, fish, shellfish or tofu. The addition of lots of fresh herbs, usually mint, coriander or basil, gets the palate zinging, adds colour and texture and helps to tame the heat of any chilli. The Thais also like to add fruit to their salads – pretty pink-fleshed pomelo, as well as mango or papaya are popular. Usually the mango and papaya are unripe (green), but you can use ripe fruit, if you prefer.

A must-have on our menu, and so a must-have in this book, is *som tam* salad (see page 202). You'll find versions of this famous fiery, refreshing green papaya salad in street-food markets and on stalls throughout Bangkok. It encapsulates the signature Thai flavours of hot, sour, salty and sweet. Although there are many different versions of *som tam*, the balance of flavours and textures is always key. The Busaba version comes with the heat from the chilli, sour from the tamarind and lime, crunch from green beans, green papaya and nuts, sweetness from the palm sugar and tomatoes, and saltiness from the fish sauce and dried shrimp. Traditionally, the salad is pounded in a large pestle and mortar, but at home a small, sharp knife,

mandolin, grater or food processor will do the job just fine. Serve and eat all our salads at room temperature, rather than fridge cold – only then will the flavours of the fresh vegetables, fruit and herbs really sing.

A classic Thai dressing is an invigorating combination of fish sauce, lime juice and/or rice or distilled vinegar, palm sugar, chilli and garlic, and is generally oil-free. Most Thai salads will come with the dressings prepared separately and served on the side. That way, the fresh salad ingredients keep their shape and crispness and don't wilt before they get to you. You can pour over just the right amount of dressing for your palate before you eat. That said, at other times a proportion of the dressing may be mixed in to allow robust ingredients to steep in the flavours and absorb them before serving. The more delicate ingredients, such as fresh herbs and leaves, are then added at the final stage with a splash more dressing.

This chapter also provides a selection of vegetable side dishes for serving alongside the curries, stir-fries and char-grilled or steamed and braised dishes in this book. They are all simple to make and will add colour, flavour and texture to your Thai feasts.

# SQUID & MANGO SALAD

In Thailand, it is common to use unripe fruit in salads. This salad is Thai in spirit in that it includes mango, but uses ripe fruit instead. The mango is combined with squid in a vibrant ginger dressing. Squid takes mere minutes to cook – any longer and it turns tough and rubbery. Don't be put off by the apparent long list of ingredients – once you've assembled them, you'll have the salad whipped up in no time at all.

**SERVES** 4
**PREP** 20 minutes, plus marinating
**COOK** 10 minutes

400g/14oz prepared squid tubes, rinsed, patted dry and cut into 1cm/½in thick rings
100g/3½oz rocket leaves
55g/2oz baby spinach leaves
1 ripe mango, peeled, stoned and cut into chunks
a handful basil leaves
a handful coriander leaves
1 medium-hot red chilli, deseeded and thinly sliced into rounds

**FOR THE MARINADE**
1 tablespoon light soy sauce
1 tablespoon cold-pressed rapeseed oil
½ teaspoon caster sugar
a large pinch of dried chilli flakes

**FOR THE DRESSING**
2cm/¾in piece of root ginger, peeled and finely chopped
1 tablespoon rice vinegar
2 garlic cloves, crushed
1–2 tablespoons fish sauce, to taste
juice of 1 lime
1 teaspoon caster sugar
1 tablespoon cold-pressed rapeseed oil
salt and freshly ground black pepper

1 Mix together the ingredients for the marinade in a large shallow dish, add the squid and turn until coated. Cover and leave to marinate in the fridge for at least 1 hour, but overnight if you have time.

2 To make the dressing, mix together all the ingredients in a non-reactive bowl with 1 tablespoon of water. Season with salt and pepper, to taste, then set aside.

3 Arrange the rocket, spinach and half of the mango on a large serving plate. Spoon a little of the dressing over and toss until lightly coated, then set aside. Remove the squid from the marinade with a slotted spoon and drain.

4 Heat a large ridged griddle pan over a high heat (or you can use a char-grill or barbecue). When hot, add half of the squid and griddle for 1½ minutes on each side, until charred in places. Place in a warm bowl and cover. Repeat with the remaining squid. Discard the marinade.

5 Arrange the squid on top of the salad and scatter over the rest of the mango, herbs and chilli. Serve straightaway with extra dressing on the side, letting everyone help themselves as they wish.

# AVOCADO & CORIANDER SUPER SALAD

This salad is simple and light, and with no cooking required takes only minutes to prepare. We've left the coriander leaves whole in our version, but you could finely chop them if you prefer.

**SERVES** 4
**PREP** 20 minutes

½ onion, finely sliced
2 spring onions, finely sliced
4cm/1½in piece of root ginger, peeled and cut into fine matchsticks
5 coriander sprigs, leaves and stalks separated, stalks sliced
4 tablespoons finely chopped roasted unsalted peanuts
3 ripe avocados, peeled, stoned and thinly sliced
juice of 1 lime
1 Thai red chilli, thinly cut into rings, to serve

**FOR THE DRESSING**
4 tablespoons distilled white vinegar
½ teaspoon caster sugar
4 tablespoons Sweet Chilli Sauce (see page 257) or sriracha sauce
salt

1  First, make the dressing. Put the vinegar in a small bowl with the sugar and a pinch of salt. Stir until the sugar dissolves, then add the sweet chilli sauce or sriracha sauce and stir again. Set aside.

2  To assemble the salad, put the onion, spring onions, ginger, coriander leaves and stalks and peanuts in a serving bowl or on a serving plate. Season with salt, to taste. Add the avocados and lime juice, then spoon over the dressing, toss gently and sprinkle with the sliced chilli to serve.

Although avocados aren't native to Thailand, the tropical climate provides perfect growing conditions for this superfruit, which as a result has been cultivated in Thailand for almost 100 years.

# CHINESE BROCCOLI

This Chinese broccoli dish is a simple vegetable stir-fry, usually cooked at home and combined with crispy pork. At Busaba (and in this recipe), we leave out the pork so that our vegetarian guests can enjoy it, too.

**SERVES** 4
**PREP** 10 minutes
**COOK** 5 minutes

2 tablespoons vegetable oil
165g/5¾oz Chinese broccoli (gai lan or kailan) or long-stem broccoli, sliced diagonally into 4cm/1½in long pieces
2 garlic cloves, finely sliced
4 shiitake mushrooms, sliced
2 tablespoons light soy sauce
a pinch of caster sugar

1 Heat a large wok or frying pan over a high heat. Add the oil and when hot, add the broccoli, garlic and shiitake and stir-fry for 2 minutes.

2 Add the soy sauce, sugar and 3 tablespoons of water and cook for another 1 minute, tossing the wok or pan as the broccoli cooks. Serve straightaway.

# WOK-FRIED PUMPKIN

Pumpkin is naturally sweet. Wok-fried with ginger and served with fresh chilli it makes a delicious accompaniment to braised Thai dishes or a substantial vegan meal in itself.

**SERVES** 4
**PREP** 10 minutes
**COOK** 15 minutes

600g/1lb 5oz pumpkin, peeled, deseeded and cut into 3cm/1¼in dice
2 tablespoons vegetable oil
2 garlic cloves, roughly chopped
4cm/1½in piece of root ginger, peeled and finely grated
1 tablespoon salted bean paste
a pinch of caster sugar
1 Thai red chilli, thinly sliced, to serve
1 small spring onion, thinly sliced, to serve

1 Steam the pumpkin for 10 minutes or until tender. Remove from the steamer and leave to cool. (You can do this up to two days in advance.)

2 Heat a large lidded wok or frying pan over a high heat. Add the oil and, when hot, add the garlic, ginger and pumpkin and stir-fry for 1 minute.

3 Add the salted bean paste and sugar and continue to stir-fry for 2 minutes, until the pumpkin is coated in the paste mixture. Pour in 100ml/3½fl oz of water, reduce the heat to medium, cover with a lid and cook for 2 minutes. Serve sprinkled with the red chilli and spring onion.

# MORNING GLORY STIR-FRY

Known as *phak bung* in Thai, and grown throughout tropical Asia, the tender shoots of water morning glory make a delicious street-food stir-fry found on every street corner in Bangkok. At night you can see the flames as vendors cast their woks into the air to toss this delicious treat.

**SERVES** 4
**PREP** 10 minutes
**COOK** 5 minutes

2 garlic cloves, crushed
2–3 Thai red chillies, thinly sliced
   into rings or left whole
2 tablespoons salted bean paste
2 teaspoons caster sugar
200g/7oz water morning glory or
   baby leaf spinach
2 tablespoons vegetable oil

1  Mix together the garlic, chillies, salted bean paste, sugar and 1 tablespoon of water in a large mixing bowl. Add the morning glory or spinach and turn until coated in the sauce.

2  Heat a large wok or frying pan over a high heat. Add the oil and when hot, add the morning glory or spinach mixture. Toss the wok, taking care as the oil can spit, for 2 minutes, until the morning glory or spinach is just tender. Remove from the heat and serve straightaway.

# MIXED ASIAN GREENS

Chinese broccoli (*gai lan* or *kailan*), white Chinese leaf and pak choi are found everywhere in the fresh Bangkok food markets. They are great vegetables cooked to accompany prawn or other fish dishes, but you can also eat them raw in salads or dip them into sweet chilli sauce as a snack.

**SERVES** 4
**PREP** 10 minutes
**COOK** 5 minutes

4 tablespoons vegetable oil
8 garlic cloves, crushed
4 Thai green chillies, halved and
   bruised
165g/5¾oz Chinese broccoli (gai lan
   or kailan) or long-stem broccoli,
   sliced diagonally into 4cm/1½in
   long pieces
165g/5¾oz Chinese leaves, leaves
   separated, sliced in half and cut
   into 3cm/1¼in diamond shapes
165g/5¾oz pak choi, leaves
   separated and cut into quarters
4 tablespoons salted bean paste
a pinch of caster sugar

1  Heat a large wok or frying pan over a high heat. Add the oil and when hot, add the garlic, chillies, Chinese broccoli, Chinese leaves and pak choi and stir-fry for 2 minutes.

2  Add the salted bean paste and sugar and stir-fry for a further 2 minutes. Pour in 4 tablespoons of water and cook for another 1 minute, tossing the wok or pan throughout, then serve straightaway.

# YAM PAK WITH CHICKEN

*Yam pak* literally means 'hot mix'. This salad gains some spiciness from the dried chilli, but it is perfectly balanced by the sweet dressing.

**SERVES** 4
**PREP** 15 minutes
**COOK** 15 minutes

2 cooked chicken breasts, shredded
1 green mango, peeled, stoned and
   shredded
2 red chicory, leaves separated and
   cut in half lengthways
2 white chicory, leaves separated
   and cut in half lengthways
1 Thai aubergine, thinly sliced
20 mint leaves
15g/½oz coriander sprigs, leaves
   and stalks separated, stalks
   sliced
3 banana shallots, finely sliced
1 tablespoon toasted coconut flakes
2 ripe avocados, peeled, stoned and
   thinly sliced
juice of 1 lime
1 tablespoon Golden Fried Shallots
   (see page 258) or ready-made
   crispy fried shallots
1 teaspoon toasted sesame seeds,
   to serve
3 whole dried chillies, toasted
   (see page 83), to serve

**FOR THE YAM PAK DRESSING**
1 tablespoon toasted sesame seeds
1 tablespoon toasted coconut flakes
100g/3½oz palm sugar or light soft
   brown sugar
50g/1¾oz tamarind concentrate
   or paste
50ml/1¾fl oz light soy sauce

1  To make the yam pak dressing, put the sesame seeds and coconut flakes in a pestle and mortar and pound until finely ground, then set aside. Alternatively, use a mini food processor or grinder. Put the sugar in a small saucepan with the light soy sauce, tamarind and 55ml/1¾fl oz of water and bring to the boil, stirring until the sugar dissolves. Reduce the heat to low, add the ground sesame seeds and coconut flakes and simmer for 10 minutes, stirring occasionally, until reduced and thickened. Remove from the heat and leave to cool.

2  Gently combine the chicken, mango and both types of chicory, along with the aubergine, mint, coriander leaves and stalks, shallots and coconut flakes in a large mixing bowl. Add 3–4 tablespoons of the dressing and toss well until combined.

3  Add the avocados, lime juice and another 3–4 tablespoons of the dressing and gently toss again until the dressing lightly coats the salad. Spoon onto a serving plate, top with the fried shallots and sprinkle with the toasted sesame seeds, then crumble over the toasted dried chillies to serve.

# PRAWN & POMELO SALAD

**Pomelo is a bit like a giant grapefruit with a delicate rose-pink flesh. Once sold only in Asian grocers, the fruit is now available to buy in most large supermarkets and greengrocers. Avocado goes really well with the prawns and pomelo and the fresh, aromatic, zingy dressing.**

**SERVES** 4
**PREP** 15 minutes

2 Little Gem lettuces, shredded
2 ripe avocados, peeled, stoned
    and cut into bite-sized chunks
½ pomelo or 1 pink grapefruit,
    peeled, segmented and
    membrane removed, then torn
    or cut into bite-sized chunks
350g/12oz cooked king or tiger
    prawns
a large handful mint leaves,
    chopped
a large handful coriander leaves,
    chopped
2 kaffir lime leaves, shredded
30g/1oz roasted unsalted peanuts,
    roughly chopped

**FOR THE DRESSING**
juice of 2 limes
3 tablespoons fish sauce
1 teaspoon caster sugar
1 medium-hot red chilli,
    deseeded and diced

**1**  Mix together all the ingredients for the dressing with 1 tablespoon of warm water, then set aside.

**2**  Arrange the shredded lettuce on a large serving plate and top with the avocados and pomelo or grapefruit, and prawns. Spoon half of the dressing over and toss lightly, then scatter over the herbs, kaffir lime leaves and peanuts. Serve straightaway, with the remaining dressing on the side, so that everyone can help themselves if they wish.

For a special twist, lobster is a delicious alternative to the prawns and you could even serve the salad in halved lobster shells.

# SOM TAM SALAD

*Som tam* is the Thai name for a papaya salad, here made with green papaya, chilli, tamarind, lime and tomatoes, and flavoured with fish sauce to give the perfect balance of sour, salty and sweet. You'll find a *som tam* shop or *som tam* street-hawker stall everywhere in Thailand, as the salad is a staple lunch dish for Thai people.

**SERVES** 2
**PREP** 20 minutes

250g/9oz green unripe papaya, peeled and seeds scooped out
2 garlic cloves, roughly chopped
2 Thai green chillies, roughly chopped
55g/2oz snake beans or fine green beans, finely sliced
55g/2oz roasted unsalted peanuts
1 tablespoon dried shrimp
8 cherry tomatoes, cut in half
2½ tablespoons palm sugar or light soft brown sugar
2 tablespoons tamarind concentrate or paste
2 tablespoons fish sauce
finely grated zest and juice of 1 lime

1  Using a sharp knife, mandolin or julienne peeler, cut the papaya into thin matchsticks and set aside.

2  Put the garlic in a large pestle and mortar and pound until crushed, then add the chillies and pound until bruised.

3  Add the beans, peanuts and dried shrimp and continue to pound for 20 seconds, then add the tomatoes and pound until everything is roughly crushed. Depending on the size of your pestle and mortar, you may need to scoop everything into a bowl at this stage.

4  Next, add the sugar, tamarind, fish sauce and finally the lime juice and zest and continue to pound until the sugar dissolves.

5  Add the papaya and pound, occasionally turning the mixture with a large spoon, until the papaya has absorbed the dressing and is lightly bruised. Remove from the mortar, if necessary, and transfer all the salad ingredients to a serving bowl, then give it all another turn until combined. Serve straightaway.

# HOT & SOUR PORK SALAD

**The combination of red curry paste, ginger and tamarind gives the marinade for this pork a fragrant, spicy hit. This is definitely a main-sized salad, although it would also work perfectly served as part of a large buffet spread. Here, we grill the pork, but you can char-grill it, if you prefer.**

**SERVES** 4
**PREP** 25 minutes, plus marinating
**COOK** 15 minutes

1 tablespoon rapeseed oil
2 tablespoons Red Curry Paste (see page 254) or ready-made paste
1 tablespoon tamarind concentrate or paste
2.5cm/1in piece of root ginger, peeled and finely grated
1 teaspoon palm sugar or light soft brown sugar
550g/1lb 4oz pork tenderloin fillet, fat and sinew trimmed, patted dry
1 small Cos lettuce, leaves separated
1 small red pepper, deseeded and cut into thin strips
½ cucumber, sliced into ribbons with a vegetable peeler, seeds discarded
2 carrots, sliced into ribbons with a vegetable peeler
4 spring onions, thinly sliced diagonally
a handful Thai basil leaves or regular basil
a handful coriander leaves
1 medium-hot red chilli, thinly sliced into rings
a handful roasted unsalted peanuts, roughly chopped
salt and ground white pepper

**FOR THE DRESSING**
1 tablespoon fish sauce
1 tablespoon light soy sauce
1 tablespoon rice vinegar
juice of 1 lime
1 teaspoon palm sugar or light soft brown sugar
1 garlic clove, crushed
1 small banana shallot, diced

1 Make a marinade by mixing together the oil, red curry paste, tamarind, ginger and sugar. Season with salt and pepper. Put the pork in a shallow dish, spoon the marinade over and rub it in to coat the meat. Cover and leave to marinate in the fridge for at least 1 hour, preferably overnight.

2 Preheat the grill to high and line the grill pan with foil. Mix together all the ingredients for the dressing with 3 tablespoons of warm water in a non-reactive bowl and set aside.

3 Place the wire grill directly on the foil in the grill pan and grill the pork for 15 minutes, turning it every 5 minutes, until golden on the outside and just cooked in the middle – there should be the merest hint of pink. Remove the meat from the grill using the foil to help you. Place the pork on a hot plate, cover with foil and leave to rest for 10 minutes.

4 To make the salad, put the lettuce on a large serving platter and arrange the red pepper, cucumber, carrots, spring onions and half the herbs on top. Spoon over half the dressing. Slice the pork into rounds and place on top of the salad, then scatter over the rest of the herbs, along with the chilli slices and chopped peanuts. Serve for everyone to help themselves with extra dressing on the side.

# DESSERTS

A Thai meal traditionally ends with simply prepared fresh tropical fruit, perfect for cleansing the palate after a meal of spicy foods and somehow countering the hot, clammy climate. In the markets of Bangkok, both on land and on water, stalls are laden with fruit of all shapes and colours – luscious mangoes, rambutan, papaya, mangosteen, star fruit, passion fruit, jackfruit and pineapples among many more. One of the most famous is durian, a strong-smelling and tasting fruit that, for most, is the fruit equivalent of a love/hate relationship (see the panel on page 219 for why). It's a seasonal fruit (the main season is during June and July) and needs eating at its peak of ripeness – in fact, in Thailand you can be prosecuted if you sell unripe durian. Although we've left it out of our fruit salad, if you do get a chance to include it, we urge you to do so, if only to measure the reactions of your guests!

Fruit aside, it's impossible to make your way around the street markets in Thailand without noticing the unending rows of perfectly formed sweet treats. Carefully manicured stalls sell a multi-coloured array of sweetmeats moulded out of sweet bean paste and glazed with sugar syrup or sprinkled with shreds of coconut. Cooked to order there are pancakes, golden battered fritters, and whole char-grilled bananas, seared until their skins blacken and the fruit softens inside. At every turn there are tropical fruit of all types steeped in a sweet and sticky syrup for eating straightaway or to take home to enjoy later the same evening (never longer – sweet-stall fare is not for keeping).

In restaurants, banana leaves, used as steaming vessels in savoury foods, become serving platters or are cleverly folded into small baskets for sweet foods. They may hold anything from sweetmeats to steamed egg custard, or jelly. Meanwhile, pandan (*Pandanus*) leaves add their distinctive vanilla flavour and vibrant green colour.

No chapter on Thai desserts would be complete without the appearance of coconut. From the water found inside a fresh coconut to coconut cream and shredded coconut, this seed–fruit lies at the heart of Thai cuisine both savoury and sweet. Here, it provides the base for a wonderful sticky rice pudding (see page 225), as well as chocolate coconut fondants (see page 212) and crème brûlées made with coconut milk (see page 213).

# BANANA FRITTERS WITH SALTED CARAMEL COCONUT SAUCE

**Complete indulgence! Banana fritters – in fact fritters in general, both sweet and savoury – are popular street food in Thailand, although you'll find the salted caramel coconut sauce is a Western addition. Choose bananas that are ripe but not too soft, as softness turns to mushiness during frying. Sprinkle over a few toasted sesame seeds before serving, or you could even add a couple of tablespoons of seeds to the batter mix.**

**SERVES** 4
**PREP** 15 minutes, plus standing
**COOK** 30 minutes

140g/5oz rice flour
75g/2½oz plain flour
1 teaspoon baking powder
2 tablespoons caster sugar
½ teaspoon salt
100ml/3½fl oz coconut milk
4 large, ripe but not too soft
    bananas, each peeled and each
    cut in half crossways, then
    lengthways to make 4 pieces
vegetable oil, for deep-frying
toasted sesame seeds, for
    sprinkling (optional)

**SALTED CARAMEL COCONUT SAUCE**
100g/3½oz light soft brown sugar
200ml/7fl oz coconut cream (could
    be from the top of the can of
    coconut milk, above), plus extra
    for serving
1 teaspoon vanilla extract
a large pinch of sea salt flakes,
    to taste

1  To make the batter for the fritters, sift both types of flour into a large mixing bowl and stir in the baking powder, sugar and salt, then make a well in the middle. With a balloon whisk, mix the coconut milk with 200ml/7fl oz of water until combined, then gradually pour it into the flour mixture, drawing it in from the sides to make a smooth thick-ish batter. Leave to stand for 20 minutes at room temperature.

2  Meanwhile, make the caramel coconut sauce. Put the sugar in a small, non-stick pan with a splash of water. Stir once, then heat gently until the sugar dissolves. Once the sugar has dissolved, cook for 1 minute, until it caramelizes slightly. Gradually, pour in the coconut cream and vanilla, stirring, then bring to a gentle boil and cook for 15 minutes, swirling the pan occasionally, until the sauce is the consistency of runny honey. Add the salt, then taste and add more salt if needed, then leave to cool slightly; it will thicken further as it cools. Set aside.

3  Pour enough oil into a large wok (use a wok stand to keep the pan stable), saucepan or deep-fat fryer to deep-fry the fritters. Heat the oil to 180°C/350°F or until a cube of day-old bread turns crisp and golden in 45 seconds.

4  Dunk 3 or 4 pieces of banana into the batter mixture until coated. Using tongs, lower them into the hot oil and deep-fry for 2–3 minutes or until crisp and golden. Carefully remove with a slotted spoon and drain on kitchen paper. Keep warm while you repeat until you've used up all the banana pieces.

5  Serve the fritters straightaway with a good drizzle of caramel coconut sauce, coconut cream and a light sprinkling of sesame seeds, if you like.

# CHOCOLATE COCONUT FONDANTS

**Admittedly, chocolate fondant isn't a typical Thai dessert, but this version has been given an Asian twist with the use of coconut, rum, cinnamon, ginger and a smidgen of chilli, which adds a slight heat. It's delicious with a spoonful of the Vanilla Coconut Cream on page 216.**

**MAKES** 4
**PREP** 20 minutes, plus chilling
**COOK** 20 minutes

150g/5½oz coconut oil, plus extra
    for greasing
150g/5½oz plain chocolate, about
    70% cocoa solids, broken into
    equal-sized pieces
1 tablespoon dark rum or coconut
    milk
150g/5½oz caster sugar
3 eggs, plus 2 egg yolks
3 tablespoons plain flour
1 teaspoon ground cinnamon
1 teaspoon ground ginger
½ medium-hot red chilli, deseeded
    and very finely chopped
Vanilla Coconut Cream (see page
    216), to serve
thinly pared zest of 1 lime,
    to decorate (optional)

1 Lightly grease four 175–200ml/6–7fl oz dariole moulds and set aside.

2 Melt the coconut oil, chocolate and rum or coconut milk in a heatproof bowl placed over a pan of gently simmering water (about 5 minutes) – make sure the bottom of the bowl does not touch the water. Leave to cool slightly.

3 Meanwhile, using an electric whisk, whisk the sugar, whole eggs and yolks in a separate mixing bowl for 3 minutes, until pale and thickened. Fold in the chocolate mixture followed by the flour, spices and chilli. Spoon the mixture into the prepared moulds and chill for 30 minutes.

4 Preheat the oven to 190°C/375°F/Gas 5 and heat a baking tray in the oven. Place the chilled fondants on the heated tray and bake for 12–14 minutes, until the sponges have risen but are still runny in the middle. Remove from the oven and leave to stand for 2 minutes.

5 Loosen the fondants from the moulds using a round-edged knife, then turn out onto serving plates. Serve the fondants with a good spoonful of the vanilla coconut cream by the side and sprinkled with lime zest, if you like.

# COCONUT CRÈME BRÛLÉES

**This simple dessert is perfect for cleansing the palate after a meal of spicy foods, especially after those made with hot Thai red chillies.**

**SERVES** 4
**PREP** 15 minutes, plus chilling
**COOK** 40 minutes

8 egg yolks
6 tablespoons caster sugar
200ml/7fl oz double cream
400ml/14fl oz can coconut milk
6 kaffir lime leaves
2 tablespoons dark soft
    brown sugar

1  Preheat the oven to 150°C/300°F/Gas 2.

2  Using an electric hand whisk, whisk the egg yolks with 4 tablespoons of the caster sugar in a large mixing bowl until pale, thick and creamy. This takes about 2 minutes.

3  Put the cream, coconut milk and kaffir lime leaves in a heavy-based saucepan and warm over a low heat, stirring occasionally, until it almost comes to the boil. Remove from the heat and leave until tepid to let the flavour of the kaffir lime leaves infuse the cream.

4  Strain the cream mixture into a jug, discarding the kaffir lime leaves, and gradually pour it into the egg yolk mixture, whisking continuously with a balloon whisk. Pour into the top of a double boiler, or a heatproof bowl set over a pan of simmering water. Heat gently, stirring, for 3 minutes or until the custard has thickened and lightly coats the back of a spoon.

5  Remove from the heat and pour the custard into four ramekins or a shallow heatproof dish. Bake for 30 minutes, until softly set and the custards still have a slight wobble in the middle. Remove from the oven and leave to cool to room temperature, then chill for 1 hour, or overnight if you prefer.

6  When ready to serve, mix the remaining 2 tablespoons caster sugar with the brown sugar and sift it over the brûlées. Spray with a little water to just dampen the top. Using a blow torch, caramelize the sugar topping, moving the flame just above the sugar. Alternatively, place the brûlées under a hot grill until the sugar melts and caramelizes, about 2 minutes. Leave the caramel topping to harden before serving.

# COCONUT CAKE WITH PINEAPPLE IN SYRUP

This light coconut cake comes with fresh pineapple steeped in
a lemongrass and ginger syrup for an indulgent sticky sweetness.
A generous spoonful of rich vanilla coconut cream by the side makes
a great alternative to regular cream.

**SERVES** 8
**PREP** 25 minutes, plus chilling
**COOK** 60 minutes

175g/6oz coconut oil, plus extra
    for greasing
40g/1½oz unsweetened desiccated
    coconut, plus extra to decorate
4 eggs, separated
175g/6oz caster sugar
a large pinch of salt
200g/7oz self-raising flour
1 teaspoon baking powder
2 x recipe quantities Lemongrass
    & Ginger Syrup (see page 219)
1 very ripe pineapple, skin and core
    discarded, cut into large
    bite-sized chunks

**FOR THE VANILLA COCONUT CREAM**
400ml/14fl oz can coconut milk,
    chilled for at least 2 hours
    before using
1 teaspoon vanilla extract
1–2 tablespoons icing sugar, sifted
a pinch of sea salt

1  First, make the coconut cream. Open the chilled can of coconut milk
and scoop out about 150g/5½oz of the thick cream on the top into a
mixing bowl, leaving the thin milk underneath. Whisk the vanilla, the
smaller quantity of icing sugar and the salt into the coconut cream until
thick. Taste and add more icing sugar, if needed, then chill until ready to
use. Stir the remaining coconut milk in the can and set aside.

2  Preheat the oven to 190°C/375°F/Gas 5. Line a 20cm/8in round cake
tin with baking paper and grease the sides with coconut oil. Measure out
170ml/5½fl oz of the reserved coconut milk into a bowl and stir in the
desiccated coconut. Set aside. Melt the coconut oil, then cool slightly.

3  Using an electric whisk, beat the egg yolks and caster sugar in a large
mixing bowl until light and creamy, about 3 minutes. Whisk in the salt,
melted coconut oil and coconut milk mixture, then fold in the flour and
baking powder. Whisk the egg whites in a separate large mixing bowl to
soft peaks. Fold a spoonful of the egg whites into the cake mixture until
combined, then gently fold in the rest of the egg whites. Transfer the
cake batter to the prepared cake tin and bake for 35–40 minutes, until
risen and golden and a skewer inserted into the middle comes out clean.
Cover the top with foil and leave the cake to cool in the tin.

4  While the cake is baking, prepare the lemongrass and ginger syrup –
see page 219, but use a medium pan, and cook for 10 minutes or until it
forms a light syrup. Discard the aromatics.

5  When the cake is cool, turn it out onto a wire rack placed over a baking
tray and remove the baking paper. Using a cocktail stick, prick small
holes all over the top of the cake. Spoon half the syrup over, letting
it soak into the cake, then generously sprinkle with extra desiccated
coconut and cut into 8 slices.

6  Add the pineapple to the remaining syrup in the pan and simmer for
5–10 minutes, occasionally spooning the syrup over the fruit, until the
syrup is golden and the pineapple has caramelized. Cool for a minute,
then spoon it over the coconut cake and serve with the coconut cream.

# TROPICAL FRUIT WITH LEMONGRASS & GINGER SYRUP

**This Thai fruit salad is brilliantly retro, and it makes a colourful end to a Thai meal. (If you want to go really retro, you could hollow out half a pineapple and serve the fruit salad in that.) Make sure all the fruit is perfectly ripe for the best flavour and serve at room temperature, rather than fridge cold. Feel free to choose your own favourite combination of fruit (perhaps even including durian), but this version is a winner.**

**SERVES** 4
**PREP** 25 minutes, plus infusing
**COOK** 5 minutes

1 pineapple
12 fresh lychees, peeled, or
    425g/15oz can, drained
½ small watermelon, deseeded,
    sliced and cut into large bite-
    sized chunks
1 papaya, cut in half, seeds scooped
    out, peeled and cut into large
    bite-sized chunks
3 mint sprigs, leaves picked,
    to decorate

**FOR THE LEMONGRASS & GINGER SYRUP**
150g/5½oz caster sugar
2 lemongrass sticks, bruised
5cm/2in piece of root ginger, cut
    into 5mm/¼in thick slices
juice of 2 limes and finely grated
    zest of 1

1  First, make the syrup. Heat 200ml/7fl oz of water in a small saucepan, then when hot add the sugar and stir until dissolved. Add the lemongrass and ginger, bring to a gentle boil and cook for 5 minutes, until it forms a light syrup. Remove from the heat and leave to cool. If you can, leave the aromatics to infuse the syrup for at least 1 hour, preferably longer.

2  Just before you are ready to use the syrup, remove and discard the aromatics and stir in the lime juice and zest.

3  To make the fruit salad, cut the pineapple in half lengthways. Take one half and make a cut around the edge, leaving a 1cm/½in border. Remove the central core, then cut the fruit into large dice and scoop out of the pineapple shell. Repeat with the second half of pineapple. (If you're planning to serve the salad inside the pineapple husks, set them aside, ready to fill.)

4  Gently mix together the pineapple chunks, lychees, watermelon and papaya in a mixing bowl, spoon over a third of the syrup and turn the fruit until coated. Transfer the fruit to a serving platter or bowl (or fill the prepared pineapple shells with the fruit mixture). Spoon over a little more of the syrup, leaving extra to serve, if needed, then decorate with mint leaves and bring to the table.

Arguably Thailand's most talked-about fruit is the durian, the so-called King of Fruits. Durian has a distinctive odour – you either love it or hate it. What some describe as putrid, others call almond-like. If you can find one, are you brave enough to try? (Beware, though, if you're a hater, the smell, even more than the taste, is hard to forget.)

# BANANA WONTONS WITH CHOCOLATE CHILLI SAUCE

Stuffed savoury wontons are hugely popular all over Asia, so why not a sweet version? Here, the wontons are filled with banana and cinnamon. They're delicious served with the rich chilli chocolate sauce.

**MAKES** 4
**PREP** 20 minutes
**COOK** 15 minutes

2 tablespoons plain flour
    or cornflour
2 ripe (but not too ripe) bananas,
    peeled and sliced into rounds,
    about 1cm/½in thick
about 1 teaspoon ground cinnamon
2 sheets filo pastry, defrosted if
    frozen and cut into
    8 x 12cm/4½in squares
vegetable oil, for deep-frying
icing sugar, for dusting

**FOR THE CHOCOLATE CHILLI SAUCE**
75g/2½oz plain chocolate, about
    70% cocoa solids, broken into
    pieces
100g/3½oz coconut cream
¼–½ teaspoon dried chilli flakes,
    to taste
2 tablespoons honey

1  First, make the chocolate chilli sauce. Put all the ingredients in a small heavy-based saucepan and heat very gently until the chocolate melts (about 5 minutes), stirring occasionally, until rich and glossy. Set aside.

2  Mix together the flour or cornflour with 2 tablespoons of water to a smooth paste – this will help to seal the edge of the wontons.

3  To assemble the wontons, take 2 squares of filo pastry and place on a worktop one on top of the other. Cover the rest of the filo with a clean, damp tea towel to stop it drying out.

4  Place 3 slices of banana in the middle of one half of the square and sprinkle over a little cinnamon. Brush the edges of the filo with the flour mixture, then fold the filo over the filling into a triangle and press the edges together to seal. Repeat with the remaining filo and filling to make 4 wontons in total.

5  Pour enough oil into a large wok (use a wok stand to keep the pan stable), saucepan or deep-fat fryer to deep-fry the wontons. Heat the oil to 180°C/350°F or until a cube of day-old bread turns crisp and golden in 45 seconds.

6  Place the wontons in the hot oil and deep-fry for 3–5 minutes or until crisp and golden. Scoop out with a slotted spoon and drain on kitchen paper. You may need to do this in two batches.

7  Warm the chocolate chilli sauce, if needed. Serve the banana wontons drizzled with the sauce or with the sauce for dipping on the side, and with a dusting of icing sugar.

# THAI BLACK RICE PUDDING

**Rice is not just a savoury side for Thai people. Many Thai dessert recipes contain jasmine rice, white sticky rice or, like here, black sticky rice.**

**SERVES** 4
**PREP** 10 minutes, plus soaking
**COOK** 40 minutes

150g/5½oz black sticky rice
300ml/10½fl oz sweetened coconut
    milk in a carton
4 tablespoons caster sugar
1 teaspoon salt
5 tablespoons thick natural yogurt
1 ripe mango, peeled, stoned and
    cut into 1cm/½in dice, to serve

1  Put the rice in a mixing bowl, pour over enough water to cover and leave to soak for 8 hours or overnight.

2  Drain the soaked black rice and place in a saucepan with the coconut milk and 300ml/10½fl oz of water and bring to the boil. Reduce the heat to medium–low and simmer, stirring often to prevent the rice sticking to the bottom of the pan, for 30 minutes or until the rice is tender but still has a little bite. Check the texture of the rice as it cooks and add extra coconut milk and water if it becomes dry.

3  Add the sugar and salt to the pan and stir until dissolved. Remove the pan from the heat, cover and leave to stand for 5 minutes.

4  Add the yogurt to the rice pudding and mix well before spooning it into four individual bowls. Top each portion with equal amounts of the mango just before serving.

> Black sticky rice (known as *kao niow dahm* in Thai) is the unhulled whole rice grain – hull it and it will become white sticky rice. Its colour is closer to dark, aubergine-like purple than true black, but it is nonetheless dramatic served up as a dessert.

# MANGO, KAFFIR LIME & LEMONGRASS SORBET

**The success of this sorbet really relies on the best-tasting ripe, luscious mangoes. If you can, buy Thai yellow mangoes with a golden skin and sweet flesh. It is now possible to buy fresh kaffir lime leaves in large supermarkets and Asian grocers, but if you can't find them, opt for frozen, rather than dried.**

**SERVES** 4
**PREP** 25 minutes, plus infusing and freezing
**COOK** 5 minutes

185g/6½oz caster sugar
2 kaffir lime leaves
2 lemongrass sticks, bruised
juice of 3 limes and finely grated zest of 2
2–3 ripe mangoes, depending on size, peeled, stoned and sliced (you need about 425g/15oz prepared fruit)
2 egg whites

1  Heat 185ml/6fl oz of water in a saucepan, then add the sugar and stir until dissolved. Add the kaffir lime leaves and lemongrass and bring the mixture to the boil. Reduce the heat slightly and simmer for 5 minutes, until it forms a light syrup. Remove from the heat and leave to cool. If you can, leave the aromatics to infuse the syrup for at least 1 hour, preferably longer.

2  Just before you are ready to use the syrup, remove and discard the aromatics and stir in the lime juice. Pour the syrup into a blender, add the mango and blend until smooth. Stir in the lime zest and egg whites.

3  Tip the mixture into an ice-cream maker or sorbetière and churn for 15 minutes or until thickened to a sorbet consistency. Transfer the sorbet to a freezer-proof container, cover and freeze for about 2 hours, until firm. If you don't have an ice-cream maker or sorbetière, spoon the mixture into a freezer-proof container with a lid. Freeze for 1 hour, until ice crystals start to form, then beat with a fork to break up the crystals and return to the freezer for another hour. Repeat a couple more times, then freeze for 2 hours, until firm.

4  Take the sorbet out of the freezer about 10–15 minutes before serving to let it soften. Serve the sorbet in scoops.

# PEANUT BUTTER & HONEYCOMB ICE CREAM

**The peanut butter adds to the rich creaminess of this indulgent ice cream, which also has chunks of chocolate-covered honeycomb flecked through it. For a double-dose of peanuts, serve a few chopped roasted nuts scattered over the top.**

**SERVES** 4
**PREP** 30 minutes, plus freezing
**COOK** 10 minutes

3 eggs
75g/2½oz caster sugar
250ml/9fl oz full-fat milk
200g/7oz good-quality peanut
    butter (smooth or crunchy)
170ml/5½fl oz sweetened
    condensed milk
150ml/5fl oz double cream
2 teaspoons vanilla extract
50g/1¾oz chocolate-covered
    honeycomb bars
a handful roasted unsalted peanuts,
    roughly chopped, to serve
    (optional)

1 Break the eggs into a large mixing bowl and add the sugar. Using an electric hand whisk, beat for 3 minutes, until pale and creamy.

2 Meanwhile, warm the milk over a low heat. Gradually, pour the warmed milk into the bowl containing the egg mixture, whisking continuously. Return the mixture to the pan and warm over a low heat, stirring, until thickened to a light custard consistency (about 5–8 minutes) – it should coat the back of a spoon.

3 Pour the custard back into the mixing bowl, whisk in the peanut butter, then the condensed milk, cream and vanilla. Leave to cool.

4 Bash the honeycomb with the end of a rolling pin into rough uneven-sized pieces and set aside.

5 Pour the peanut butter custard into an ice-cream maker and churn for about 15 minutes or until you have an ice-cream consistency. (You may need to do this in two batches.) Fold in the honeycomb, then spoon the mixture into a freezer-proof container, cover and freeze until firm. If you don't have an ice-cream maker, pour the mixture into a freezer-proof container, cover with a lid and freeze. Whisk or blend after 1 hour to break up any ice crystals, then repeat twice more and freeze until firm.

6 Remove the ice cream from the freezer about 10 minutes before serving to let it soften. Serve in scoops topped with a sprinkling of peanuts, if you like.

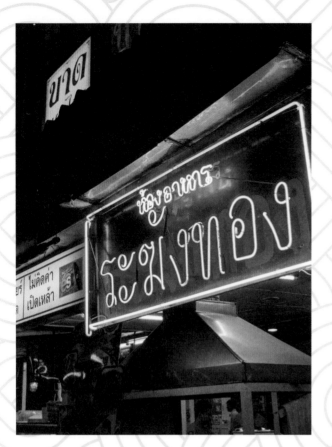

# SNACKS & DRINKS

At Busaba, the drinks' menu is inspired by the latest scene in the coolest, chicest bars, restaurants and cafés of Bangkok. This Asian mega-city has some of the most glamorous hotel roof-top bars in the world, where guests are treated to panoramic views while sipping cocktails and listening to live music. But if crowded bar-life isn't your scene, take to the mobile cocktail bars, which change location on a regular basis to keep guests (and the authorities) on their toes.

For lovers of rum, whisky or gin, specialist independent bars are popping up all over the city, serving a collection of cocktails made in interesting and creative combinations, always beautifully served in chilled glasses or cups and lavished with garnishes.

Rock up in a bar and you'll find the drinks' menu comes with a menu for bar snacks, too. These single-plate dishes or nibbles help to give the stomach something to cling onto through the bite of the spirits, while their intense spiciness stimulates the palate as well as the thirst.

That's not to say it's all about the alcohol. Freshly squeezed fruit juices made from lime, orange and pineapple or a combination of tropical fruit provide refreshing respite in easygoing cafés or from smiling street vendors as you weave your way through the markets. For the ultimate ready-made drink, you can't beat coconut water sucked through a straw from the coconut husk itself.

Lassis are as popular in Thailand as they are in India. Reputed to be the world's first smoothie, the sweet, creamy lassi is the perfect foil to spicy food: the combination of natural yogurt, coconut milk and/or buttermilk is ideal for cooling the mouth and calming the stomach. Mango and banana make a particularly good combo, but make sure you use fruit at the peak of ripeness for the best flavour. There are savoury lassis, too, which are salted and flavoured with spices such as cumin and turmeric.

Cooling long drinks of iced tea and iced coffee are big in Thailand and come with or without the addition of spices such as cardamom, cloves, cinnamon, star anise and tamarind. Tea is served black (strongly brewed Ceylon tea) or with sweetened condensed milk, and possibly evaporated milk, and for an extra sweet tooth with sugar or sugar syrup. For the ultimate caffeine hit, though, Thais like to combine tea (usually red) and coffee together.

# TEMPURA GREEN BEANS

**Green beans deep fried in tempura batter and nibbled on over cocktails. We can't think of anything better to accompany an apéritif.**

**SERVES** 4
**PREP** 15 minutes
**COOK** 15 minutes

80g/2¾oz rice flour
vegetable oil, for deep-frying
250g/9oz green beans, trimmed

**FOR THE TEMPURA BATTER**
40g/1½oz self-raising flour
1 teaspoon salt
1 teaspoon ground white pepper
1 teaspoon ground coriander
2 teaspoons caster sugar
1 teaspoon dried chilli flakes

1  To make the tempura batter, mix all the ingredients together in a bowl, then make a well in the middle. Gradually pour in 150ml/5fl oz of water and whisk to draw the dry ingredients into the wet to make a batter. Set aside until ready to use. Put the rice flour in a separate mixing bowl.

2  Pour enough oil into a large wok (use a wok stand to keep the pan stable), saucepan or deep-fat fryer to deep-fry the beans. Heat the oil to 180°C/350°F or until a cube of day-old bread turns crisp and golden in 45 seconds. When the oil is hot, dunk a few of the beans into the rice flour, then into the batter until coated all over.

3  Place the beans into the hot oil, a small handful at a time, and deep-fry for 3 minutes, turning once until crisp and golden brown. Scoop out with a slotted spoon and drain on kitchen paper, then serve while still warm.

# MATCHSTICK CHICKEN DIPS

**In the restaurants we offer up matchstick chicken wings, but for cooking at home, thighs are easier. The results are equally delicious.**

**SERVES** 4
**PREP** 10 minutes, plus marinating
**COOK** 15 minutes

4 boneless, skinless chicken thighs,
    sliced into thin strips
2 tablespoons fish sauce
vegetable oil, for deep-frying
Sweet Chilli Sauce (see page 257)
    or sriracha sauce, to serve

1  Put the chicken in a large mixing bowl, pour over the fish sauce and turn until combined. Leave to marinate for 10–15 minutes (any longer and the chicken will become too salty).

2  Pour enough oil into a large wok (use a wok stand to keep the pan stable), saucepan or deep-fat fryer to deep-fry the chicken. Heat the oil to 180°C/350°F or until a cube of day-old bread turns crisp and golden in 45 seconds. Remove the chicken from the marinade. Place in the hot oil, one piece at a time, and deep-fry for 5 minutes, turning once until crisp golden brown and cooked. Cook a small handful of chicken strips at a time and continue until all the chicken is cooked. Scoop out with a slotted spoon and drain on kitchen paper. Place on a serving plate and serve warm with the sweet chilli sauce or sriracha sauce on the side.

# SPICED CRAB DIP WITH WONTON CHIPS

**Quick and easy to prepare, this crab dip is flavoured with red curry paste. Wonton chips and crudités are perfect for scooping and dunking, while chatting to friends over a drink.**

**SERVES** 4
**PREP** 10 minutes
**COOK** 10 minutes

1½ tablespoons rapeseed oil
2 large garlic cloves, finely chopped
5cm/2in piece of root ginger, peeled and finely chopped
2 teaspoons Red Curry Paste (see page 254) or ready-made paste
200g/7oz mixed white and brown crabmeat
juice of 1 lime
1 tablespoon chopped coriander leaves
selection of fresh vegetable crudités, such as carrot, cucumber, red pepper, sugar snap peas, to serve
lime wedges, to serve
salt and ground white pepper

**FOR THE WONTON CHIPS**
8 wonton wrappers for frying, defrosted if frozen
rapeseed oil, for brushing
1 teaspoon black sesame seeds, for sprinkling

1  To make the wonton chips, preheat the oven to 180°C/350°F/Gas 4. Lightly brush both sides of each wonton wrapper with oil and place on a baking sheet. Sprinkle the sesame seeds over and bake for 5–7 minutes, until light golden. Remove from the heat and leave to cool on a wire rack.

2  To make the dip, heat a wok or frying pan over a medium heat. Add the oil, garlic and ginger and stir-fry for 1 minute, then stir in the red curry paste and cook for another 1 minute. Transfer to a serving bowl and leave to cool.

3  Stir the crabmeat, lime juice and coriander leaves into the bowl and season with salt and pepper, to taste. Serve the crab dip with a selection of vegetable crudités and the wonton chips, and lime wedges on the side.

# SUGAR & SPICE ROASTED CASHEWS

The perfect accompaniment to pre-dinner drinks, these cashews are coated in a combination of coconutty sugar syrup and spices, then roasted until golden. If your chilli powder is particularly hot you may wish to use a smaller quantity than suggested here – or not!

**MAKES** 300g/10½oz
**PREP** 10 minutes
**COOK** 25 minutes

4 teaspoons caster sugar
4 teaspoons coconut oil
1 teaspoon sea salt
⅔ teaspoon 5-spice powder
⅔ teaspoon chilli powder,
    or to taste
300g/10½oz cashew nuts
chilli flakes, to serve (optional)

1  Preheat the oven to 170°C/325°F/Gas 3. Line two large baking trays with baking paper.

2  Put the sugar and 2 tablespoons of water in a small saucepan. Heat over a medium heat, stirring until the sugar dissolves, then gently boil for about 2 minutes or until it forms a syrup. Stir in the coconut oil and heat until melted, then remove the pan from the heat.

3  Mix together the salt, 5-spice and chilli powder in a medium mixing bowl, add the cashews and mix well until the nuts are coated in the spice mix. Pour the coconut oil mixture over and stir until everything is well combined. Tip the nuts onto the prepared baking trays and spread them out in an even layer.

4  Roast the nuts for 17–20 minutes, until light golden – turn the nuts and swap the trays round halfway through so they cook evenly. Remove from the oven and leave the cashews to cool. Transfer the nuts to serving bowls with chilli flakes on the side for sprinkling, if you wish.

# MIANG KHAM

The name *miang kham* means 'one-bite wrap'. Here, the combination of peanuts, fresh prawns (rather than the more usual dried), coconut, pineapple and chilli with a shrimp paste and ginger relish will pep up your taste buds ready for the main event. If you can't find miang leaves, there are plenty of alternatives – try steamed cabbage leaves, or raw spinach, chicory or radicchio leaves, or crisp lettuce leaves.

**MAKES** 16
**PREP** 20 minutes
**COOK** 10 minutes

16 miang leaves or alternative (see recipe introduction), washed and patted dry
16 large cooked king or tiger prawns, about 150g/5½oz total weight
1 banana shallot, diced
125g/4½oz diced pineapple
40g/1½oz toasted unsalted peanuts, roughly chopped
2 medium-hot red chillies, deseeded and thinly sliced
3 tablespoons roughly chopped coriander leaves
2 tablespoons toasted unsweetened desiccated coconut

**FOR THE SHRIMP & GINGER RELISH**
2 teaspoons shrimp paste
2.5cm/1in piece of root ginger, peeled and finely chopped
2.5cm/1in piece of galangal, peeled and finely chopped
2 large lemongrass sticks, peeled and finely chopped
2 tablespoons fish sauce
125g/4½oz light muscovado sugar

1  First make the shrimp and ginger relish. Heat the shrimp paste in a small dry saucepan over a low heat for 1 minute, stirring, then add the rest of the ingredients. Stir well and cook over a medium–low heat for 8 minutes, stirring, or until thickened to a sticky paste. Add a splash of hot water if the relish is too thick – it should be the consistency of a chutney. Spoon the relish into a bowl and leave to cool.

2  To assemble the miang kham, place a miang leaf on a worktop and place a prawn in the centre. Sprinkle over a little each of the shallot, pineapple and peanuts, then top with a small spoonful of the relish. Finish by sprinkling over a little chilli, coriander and coconut. Repeat to make 16 miang kham in total.

3  To serve, either arrange the filled leaves on a large serving platter or fold into a cone-shape and place in a small shot glass or cup. Fold the leaf over before eating to hold in the filling.

# MEKHONG FLIP

**Although often referred to as 'Thai whiskey', Mekhong Thai Spirit is basically a flavoured rum, available from speciality spirit stores and online. It is a beautiful golden, caramel colour with sweet, nutty flavours. If you can't get hold of it, substitute with your favourite flavoured rum.**

**SERVES** 1
**PREP** 5 minutes

40ml/1½fl oz Mekhong Thai Spirit or other dark rum, such as Captain Morgan Spiced Gold or Havana Club Especial
2 teaspoons Cointreau
15ml/½fl oz pineapple syrup
a pinch of ground mixed spice, plus extra to decorate (optional)
1 egg
pineapple leaf, to decorate (optional)

1  Pour all the ingredients up to the mixed spice into a Boston cocktail shaker. Add the mixed spice, crack in the egg and shake vigorously for 10 seconds to combine. Open the shaker and pour the contents into the top half.

2  Three-quarters fill the larger bottom half of the shaker with ice and carefully place the two parts together again, tipping in the ice as you do. Secure and shake again for 10 seconds, then strain into a coupette glass (a hawthorne strainer is ideal for this).

3  Sprinkle a pinch of ground spice along the length of the pineapple leaf, if using, then balance the leaf across the top of the glass before serving.

# ROSELLE COLLINS

**The beautiful hibiscus flower grows throughout Asia and its syrup (available in most supermarkets or drinks outlets) lends a gentle floral note and glorious red colour to this Vodka Collins.**

**SERVES** 1
**PREP** 5 minutes

50ml/1¾fl oz vodka
1 tablespoon hibiscus syrup
25ml/1fl oz lemon and lime juice
20ml/⅔fl oz lemongrass syrup
50ml/1¾fl oz soda water
50ml/1¾fl oz prosecco
banana leaf and hibiscus flower, to decorate (optional)

1  Pour all the ingredients except the soda water and prosecco into the top half of a Boston cocktail shaker.

2  Three-quarters fill the larger bottom half of the shaker with ice and carefully place the two parts together. Secure and shake vigorously for 10 seconds, then strain into a large balloon wine glass (a hawthorne strainer is ideal for this). Top up with the soda water and prosecco.

3  Decorate with a banana leaf and hibiscus flower, to serve, if you wish.

# SANGSOM RUM & BITTERS

**Aged in charred oak barrels, this special Thai rum has a deep smoky flavour. The red wine gives the cocktail a port-like, warming feel.**

**SERVES** 1
**PREP** 5 minutes

50ml/1¾fl oz SangSom Thai rum or other dark rum, such as Captain Morgan Spiced Gold or Havana Club Especial
20ml/⅔fl oz Baltasar Gracián Red wine or other Spanish red grenache
2 dashes Angostura Bitters
orange slice and cinnamon stick, to decorate

1 Pour all the ingredients into a mixing glass. Add ice to the glass until it is three-quarters full and stir quickly for about 15 seconds to combine and thoroughly chill the ingredients.

2 Add fresh ice cubes to a rocks glass or short tumbler, then strain the cocktail into the glass (a julep strainer is ideal for this).

3 Place the orange slice and cinnamon stick in the glass, then carefully light the tip of the cinnamon until it starts to smoke; the smoke will die off after a few minutes leaving only a wonderful cinnamon aroma.

# BUSABA & MARY

**Cure the morning-after feeling the Busaba way with our Thai rum take on a classic vodka-based Bloody Mary.**

**SERVES** 1
**PREP** 5 minutes

50ml/1¾fl oz vodka or Mekhong Thai Spirit or other dark rum, such as Captain Morgan Spiced Gold or Havana Club Especial
25ml/1fl oz lemon juice
50ml/1¾fl oz Bloody Mary Spicer or similar mix
125ml/4fl oz tomato juice
lemon wedge
lemongrass salt or regular salt
banana leaf, prawn cracker, dried nori flake, sriracha sauce and slice of fresh mango, to decorate

1 Pour all the liquid ingredients into the top half of a Boston cocktail shaker, then add about 10 ice cubes. Strain into the larger bottom half of the shaker (a julep strainer is ideal for this). Pour the cocktail from one half of the shaker to the other (known as rolling) six further times.

2 Take the lemon wedge and wipe it around the rim of a highball glass or tall tumbler. Sprinkle the lemongrass salt or regular salt onto a small plate and dunk the rim of the glass into it until lightly coated.

3 Place a banana leaf in the glass and add extra ice. Strain the cocktail into the glass and decorate with the prawn cracker and nori flake, then drizzle a little sriracha sauce on top. Finally, add the mango slice.

## PROVINCE 76

Infusing any liqueur with aromatics gives endless possibilities when it comes to cocktail flavour combinations. This cocktail begins with making cardamom-infused Campari.

**SERVES** 1
**PREP** 5 minutes, plus infusing

35ml/1¼fl oz tablespoons Campari
1 Thai cardamom pod or green cardamom, seeds ground
15ml/½fl oz sweet red vermouth
15ml/½fl oz dry white vermouth
150ml/5fl oz Asahi Japanese beer
a few chives and an orange slice, to decorate

1  First, make cardamom-infused Campari. Put the Campari in a small saucepan with the cardamom and warm over a low heat for 1 minute; do not let it boil. Remove from the heat and leave to infuse for 30 minutes, then strain and leave to cool.

2  Pour all the ingredients except the Asahi and the chives and orange slice into a highball glass or tall tumbler and stir once. Three-quarters fill with ice and top up with the Asahi.

3  To decorate, place the orange slice on the edge of the glass. Take a few chives and tie a knot in the bottom, then place in the cocktail behind the orange.

## MANGO, HONEY & CARDAMOM LASSI

Of course, not every drink on a Bangkok bar menu is an alcoholic cocktail. Fruity and creamy, the lassi is famously good at cooling the mouth while eating a spicy meal or bar snack. Make sure to use a lovely ripe mango for the best flavour.

**MAKES** 4
**PREP** 10 minutes

2 large ripe mangoes, destoned
500ml/17fl oz thick natural yogurt
3–4 Thai cardamom or green cardamom pods, seeds ground
1 tablespoon runny honey
300ml/10½fl oz buttermilk or water
juice of 1 lime
ground cinnamon, for sprinkling
mango slices and banana leaf, to decorate (optional)

1  Roughly chop the mango flesh and put it in a blender with the yogurt, ground cardamom seeds, honey, buttermilk or water, and lime juice, then blend until smooth and creamy.

2  Place a few ice cubes in each glass, pour in the lassi and sprinkle over a little cinnamon before serving. You can decorate each serving with a slice of mango and a banana leaf, too, if you wish.

# GINGER & MINT ICED JASMINE TEA

**Fragrant and light, jasmine tea is best bought loose as 'pearls', when the young green tea leaves are rolled into small balls with jasmine blossom. Infused with lemongrass and ginger and topped with soda to serve long, this makes a refreshing, cooling antidote to the Bangkok heat.**

**SERVES** 4
**PREP** 10 minutes, plus infusing and chilling

2 large lemongrass sticks, bruised
8cm/3¼in piece of root ginger, cut into 5mm/¼in thick rounds
1 tablespoon loose jasmine tea
2 tablespoons runny honey, or to taste
a handful mint leaves
chilled soda water, to serve
bamboo leaf, to decorate

1  Pour 800ml/28fl oz of just-boiled water into a heatproof bowl, add the lemongrass, ginger and tea, stir well to combine and leave to cool and infuse for 1 hour.

2  When cool, strain the tea into a jug. Pick the ginger and lemongrass out of the sieve and return them to the strained tea, then stir in the honey. Taste for sweetness and add more honey, if you like, then place in the fridge to chill.

3  To serve, fill each glass with ice and add a few mint leaves. Strain the tea into the glasses, top with soda, and add a bamboo leaf, to decorate.

# THAI ICED COFFEE WITH CARDAMOM

**Versions of this spiced coffee are served in most markets and cafés in Thailand. It makes a cooling, reviving drink on a hot, sticky day. You could substitute the coffee for black or green tea, if you prefer. Some cafés will even serve you up a coffee-and–tea combo!**

**SERVES** 4
**PREP** 10 minutes, plus chilling

1 litre/35fl oz strong ready-made coffee
6 Thai cardamom or green cardamom pods, bruised
2 cinnamon sticks, plus extra to serve
6 cloves
125ml/4fl oz chilled sweetened condensed milk
4 tablespoons extra thick cream or whipped cream, to serve (optional)

1  Prepare the coffee the way you like it (ground and strong is preferable) and pour it into a jug while still hot. Stir in the cardamom pods, cinnamon sticks and cloves. Leave the mixture to cool, then place in the fridge for at least 1 hour or overnight, if time allows, to let the aromatics infuse the coffee.

2  Just before serving, strain the cooled coffee, discarding the aromatics. Put a few ice cubes in each glass, pour in equal amounts of the coffee and stir 1 tablespoon of the condensed milk into each serving. Add a second tablespoon of condensed milk to each glass, but let it sink to the bottom (it should have a layered appearance). Add a spoonful of cream on top, if using, and a cinnamon stick for stirring. Serve straightaway.

# PASTES
## SAUCES & SIDES

# THAI FOOD FUNDAMENTALS

This chapter may seem a hodge-podge of recipes, but the one thing they all have in common is that they add that extra something to your Thai cooking – a burst of colour, or flavour, or texture. Over the following pages, you'll find a selection of our favourite curry pastes (the all-important foundation of Thai curries); hot-and-sour sauces that you can add to and serve with your dishes; accompaniments, such as crispy fried shallots, to be sprinkled over a meal before serving; and let's not forget the prized centre of every meal – rice.

Traditionally, condiments, relishes and sauces play an important part of a Thai meal, complementing the main dishes but also allowing you to tailor your meal to suit your own tastes, whether it be to ramp-up chilli levels with a Chilli Jam (see page 258) or Sweet Chilli Sauce (see page 257), or cool things down with a palate-calming cucumber relish (see, for example, page 32).

For a truly traditional cooking experience, you'll need to pound the ingredients of your curry pastes in a large pestle and mortar, adding ingredients one by one and then grinding until smooth. The work is painstaking, but it creates a paste with the best flavour and consistency. That said, a

mini food processor or grinder will do the job in a fraction of the time and – we get it – is probably more practical.

Whatever method you choose, we are confident that making your own pastes and sauces will mean that not only are they free from additives, the end results – packed with fresh ingredients and aromatic herbs and spices – taste better than shop-bought alternatives, too. Make in batches (these recipes will make enough to last for a few meals) and store them in an airtight container or jar. Sauces will keep like this in the fridge for up to a month, and pastes for up to two weeks, so you don't need to make fresh every time. Avoid freezing them, though, as this negatively affects their flavour.

Don't feel you have to stick to using these pastes and sauces in curries alone. They are much more versatile than you may think – a spoonful of paste is a simple way to lift the flavour of a burger (see page 163), add oomph to a marinade or dressing, or lend a new dimension to an otherwise mild-tasting dish.

Finally, this chapter includes our recipes for making sides of perfect jasmine rice and sweet-tasting coconut rice (see page 259), which are the staples you need at every Thai feast.

# RED CURRY PASTE

**MAKES** about 200g/7oz
**PREP** 20 minutes, plus soaking
**COOK** less than 5 minutes

20g/¾oz dried Thai red chillies
3 tablespoons coriander seeds
1½ teaspoons cumin seeds
3 lemongrass sticks, peeled and roughly chopped
6 garlic cloves
1 banana shallot, chopped
5 kaffir lime leaves, thinly sliced
3cm/1¼in piece of galangal, peeled and
    roughly chopped
1½ teaspoons roughly chopped krachai
    (wild ginger), optional
1½ teaspoons roughly chopped coriander roots
a large pinch of salt

1  Put the chillies in a large heatproof mixing bowl
and pour over enough just-boiled water from a kettle
to cover. Leave to soak overnight until softened, then
drain. Roughly chop the chillies.

2  Put the coriander seeds and cumin seeds in a large
dry wok or frying pan and toast over a medium–low
heat, tossing the pan occasionally, for about 1 minute
or until the spices start to smell aromatic. Transfer
to a large pestle and mortar and grind to a coarse
powder. Alternatively, use a mini food processor or
grinder.

3  Gradually add the chillies, and the rest of the
ingredients one by one, and pound to make a smooth
paste. Alternatively, put all the ingredients in the
mini food processor or grinder – you may need to
add a tablespoon of water – and blitz to a paste.
The paste will keep for up to 2 weeks stored in the
fridge in an airtight container.

# GREEN CURRY PASTE

**MAKES** about 200g/7oz
**PREP** 15 minutes
**COOK** less than 5 minutes

2 teaspoons coriander seeds
40g/1½oz Thai green chillies
20g/¾oz piece of galangal, peeled and finely chopped
2 lemongrass sticks, peeled and finely chopped
6 kaffir lime leaves, finely chopped
10 coriander stalks
6 garlic cloves, finely chopped
1 large banana shallot, chopped
3 pinches of salt
finely grated zest of 1 lime
30g/1oz shrimp paste (optional – leave out if you are
    vegetarian or vegan)

1  First, toast the coriander seeds. Put them in a dry
wok or frying pan and toast over a medium–low heat,
tossing the pan occasionally, until the spices start
to smell aromatic. This will take about 2 minutes.
Transfer the seeds to a large pestle and mortar and
grind to a coarse powder. Alternatively, use a mini
food processor or grinder. Set aside.

2  Put the chillies, galangal, lemongrass, kaffir limes
leaves, coriander stalks, garlic and shallot in a mini
food processor or blender. Add the salt and blend
for 5 minutes or until it forms a smooth paste. Add
the lime zest, ground coriander and shrimp paste, if
using, and blend again. The paste will keep for up to
1 week stored in the fridge in an airtight container.

# YELLOW CURRY PASTE

**MAKES** about 225g/8oz
**PREP** 20 minutes, plus soaking

20g/¾oz dried Thai red chillies, soaked overnight
 and drained
1 teaspoon cloves, broken
1 teaspoon cumin seeds
4 tablespoons mild curry powder
50g/1¾oz piece of galangal, peeled and finely chopped
1 teaspoon ground nutmeg
3 lemongrass sticks, peeled and chopped
2 teaspoons ground turmeric
1 large banana shallot
2 teaspoons salt

1  Roughly chop the soaked chillies, then put
them in a bowl and, one by one, add the remaining
ingredients except the salt, pounding the mixture
between each addition.

2  Add the salt and pound again until you have a
smooth paste. Alternatively, put all the ingredients
in a mini food processor or grinder and blitz to a
paste. The paste will keep for up to 2 weeks stored
in the fridge in an airtight container.

# MASSAMAN CURRY PASTE

**MAKES** about 150g/5½oz
**PREP** 10 minutes, plus soaking
**COOK** less than 5 minutes

30g/1oz dried Thai red chillies
1 teaspoon coriander seeds
1 teaspoon aniseed seeds
1 teaspoon cloves
1 teaspoon cumin seeds
½ cinnamon stick, roughly broken
2 Thai cardamom or green cardamom pods, deseeded
1 small banana shallot, chopped
6 garlic cloves
2.5cm/1in piece of galangal, peeled and roughly chopped
1 large lemongrass stick, peeled and roughly chopped
2 teaspoons roughly chopped coriander roots
a large pinch of salt and freshly ground black pepper

1  Put the chillies in a large heatproof mixing bowl
and pour over enough just-boiled water from a kettle
to cover. Leave to soak overnight until softened, then
drain. Roughly chop the chillies.

2  Put the coriander seeds, aniseeds, cloves, cumin,
cinnamon and cardamom in a large dry wok or frying
pan and toast over a medium–low heat, tossing the
pan occasionally, for about 1 minute or until the
spices start to smell aromatic. Transfer to a large
pestle and mortar and grind to a coarse powder.
Alternatively, use a mini food processor or grinder.

3  Gradually, add the chillies and the rest of the
ingredients, one by one, and pound to make a
smooth paste. Alternatively, put all the ingredients
in the mini food processor or grinder – you may need
to add a tablespoon of water – and blitz to a paste.
The paste will keep for up to 2 weeks stored in the
fridge in an airtight container.

# SONGKHLA CURRY PASTE

**MAKES** about 250g/9oz
**PREP** 20 minutes, plus soaking
**COOK** less than 5 minutes

30g/1oz dried Thai red chillies
1 tablespoon cumin seeds
1 tablespoon cloves
50g/1¾oz piece of galangal, peeled and finely chopped
2 lemongrass sticks, peeled and finely chopped
10g/¼oz coriander stalks, chopped
2 garlic cloves, finely chopped
1 Thai red chilli, roughly chopped
100g/3½oz Red Curry Paste (see page 254)
   or ready-made paste

1  Put the chillies in a large heatproof mixing bowl and pour over enough just-boiled water from a kettle to cover. Leave to soak overnight until softened, then drain. Roughly chop the chillies.

2  Put the cumin seeds and cloves in a dry wok or frying pan and toast over a medium–low heat, tossing the pan occasionally, for about 1 minute or until the spices smell aromatic. Transfer to a large pestle and mortar and grind to a coarse powder. Alternatively, use a mini food processor or grinder.

3  Gradually add the chillies, and the rest of the ingredients one by one, and pound to make a smooth paste. Stir in the red curry paste. Alternatively, put all the ingredients in the mini food processor or grinder and blitz to a paste. The paste will keep for up to 2 weeks stored in the fridge in an airtight container.

# PAD THAI SAUCE

**MAKES** about 300ml/10½fl oz
**PREP** 5 minutes
**COOK** 20 minutes

100g/3½oz tamarind concentrate or paste
75g/2½oz palm sugar or light soft brown sugar
a pinch of salt
1 tablespoon distilled white vinegar

1  Mix together all the ingredients in a medium saucepan with 250ml/9fl oz of water and bring to the boil.

2  Reduce the heat to a simmer and cook for 20 minutes, until reduced and thickened. Stir the sauce occasionally to stop it sticking to the bottom of the pan. The sauce will keep for up to 2 weeks stored in the fridge in an airtight container

# SWEET CHILLI SAUCE

**MAKES** about 200ml/7fl oz
**PREP** 10 minutes, plus soaking
**COOK** 20 minutes

10g/¼oz medium-hot dried red chillies, deseeded
135ml/4½fl oz rice vinegar
75g/2½oz palm sugar or light soft brown sugar
6 garlic cloves, roughly chopped
2.5cm/1in piece of root ginger, peeled
   and roughly chopped
2 tablespoons groundnut oil
1 Thai red chilli, deseeded and finely chopped
1 tablespoon fish sauce
1 tablespoon light soy sauce
1 teaspoon sesame oil
salt

1  Put the dried chillies in a heatproof bowl and pour over enough hot water to cover. Cover the bowl and leave to soak for at least 1 hour.

2  Heat the vinegar and sugar in a small pan over a medium heat, stirring, until the sugar dissolves, then simmer for 5 minutes, until it forms a light syrup.

3  Meanwhile, drain the chillies and blitz them in a mini food processor with the garlic, ginger and groundnut oil to a coarse paste.

4  Add the chilli purée to the pan with the fresh chilli, fish sauce, soy sauce and sesame oil. Bring to the boil, then turn the heat down slightly and cook over a gentle rolling boil for 15 minutes, until reduced and thickened. Season with salt to taste. Leave to cool, then spoon the sauce into a sterilized jar with a lid. The sauce will keep in the fridge for up to 1 month.

# SWEET CHILLI
# TOMATO SAUCE

**MAKES** about 500ml/17fl oz
**PREP** 10 minutes
**COOK** 20 minutes

1 large Thai red chilli, finely chopped
200ml/7fl oz distilled white vinegar
40g/1½oz palm sugar or soft light brown sugar
a pinch of salt
450g/1lb caster sugar
2 tablespoons tomato ketchup

1  Place all the ingredients in a small saucepan with 200ml/7fl oz of water, stir well and bring to the boil.

2  Reduce the heat to low and simmer for 20 minutes, stirring regularly, or until the sauce has reduced and thickened. Leave to cool, then spoon the sauce into lidded sterilized jar(s). It will keep in the fridge for up to 1 month. (If you are vegetarian or vegan, you can use this sauce in place of Sweet Chilli Sauce in any of the recipes in the book.)

# CHILLI JAM

**MAKES** about 250ml/9fl oz
**PREP** 10 minutes, plus soaking
**COOK** 20 minutes

100g/3½oz large dried chillies, deseeded
2 tablespoons sunflower or olive oil
6 garlic cloves, finely chopped
2.5cm/1in piece of root ginger, peeled
    and finely chopped
1 banana shallot, finely chopped
3 Thai red chillies, deseeded
30g/1oz palm sugar or light soft brown sugar
salt and ground white pepper

1  Put the dried chillies in a large heatproof bowl and
pour over enough hot water to cover. Cover the bowl
and leave to soak for at least 1 hour, until softened,
then drain. Roughly chop the chillies.

2  Heat the oil in a medium saucepan over a low heat.
Add the garlic, ginger and shallot and cook, stirring,
for 1 minute.

3  Add the fresh and rehydrated chillies to the
pan and cook for another 1 minute, stirring.

4  Add the sugar and pour in enough water to cover.
Bring to the boil, then reduce the heat and simmer
for 20 minutes, until the chillies have softened and
start to break down.

5  Remove from the heat, leave to cool slightly, then
transfer to a blender. Blend briefly to a chunky jam
consistency. Season with salt and pepper, to taste.
Leave to cool, then spoon the jam into a sterilized
jar with a lid. The jam will keep in the fridge for up
to 1 month.

# GOLDEN FRIED SHALLOTS

**MAKES** about 100g/3½oz
**PREP** 5 minutes
**COOK** 10 minutes

200ml/7fl oz vegetable oil
3 banana shallots, very thinly sliced

1  Heat the oil in a medium wok or frying pan over
a high heat. When hot, slowly add the shallots and
stir-fry for 8 minutes, until golden and crisp.

2  Using a slotted spoon, scoop out the shallots and
drain on kitchen paper. Leave to cool and crisp up
further. (It may be worth cooking double the amount
as the shallots will keep in an airtight container in
the fridge for up to 1 week.)

**Variations**
You can use this technique to make golden fried
garlic, onion and ginger, too:

- **GOLDEN FRIED GARLIC** Thinly slice 6 garlic cloves and
  fry following the instructions, above, for 1 minute
  or until just starting to colour. Take care as you
  don't want the garlic to burn as it can turn bitter.
  Using a slotted spoon, scoop out and drain on
  kitchen paper.
- **GOLDEN FRIED ONION** Very thinly slice 1 large onion
  and fry following the instructions, above, for
  8 minutes or until golden and crisp. Using a slotted
  spoon, scoop out and drain on kitchen paper.
- **GOLDEN FRIED GINGER** Cut a 5cm/2in piece of peeled
  fresh root ginger into thin matchsticks and fry
  following the instructions, above, for 3 minutes or
  until light golden and crisp. Using a slotted spoon,
  scoop out and drain on kitchen paper.

# PERFECT JASMINE RICE

**SERVES** 4
**PREP** 5 minutes
**COOK** 15 minutes

300g/10½oz jasmine rice
a large pinch of salt

1  Rinse the rice in a sieve under cold running water until the water runs clear, then drain.

2  Tip the rice into a medium saucepan and pour in 500ml/17fl oz of cold water; it should cover the rice by about 1cm/½in. Season with the salt, stir and bring to the boil.

3  Reduce the heat to the lowest setting, cover the pan with a lid and simmer for 12–15 minutes or until the grains are soft and fluffy and the liquid has been absorbed. (This is the absorption method of cooking rice, so there's no need to drain it afterwards.)

4  Remove the pan from the heat and leave the rice to sit for 5 minutes, then fluff it up with a fork before serving.

# COCONUT RICE

**SERVES** 4
**PREP** 5 minutes
**COOK** 15 minutes

300g/10½oz jasmine rice
200ml/7fl oz coconut milk
a large pinch of salt

1  Rinse the rice in a sieve under cold running water until the water runs clear, then drain.

2  Tip the rice into a medium saucepan and pour in 300ml/10½fl oz of cold water and the coconut milk; the liquid should cover the rice by about 1cm/½in. Season with the salt, stir and bring to the boil.

3  Reduce the heat to the lowest setting, cover the pan with a lid and simmer for 12–15 minutes or until the grains are soft and fluffy and the liquid has been absorbed.

4  Remove the pan from the heat and leave the rice to sit for 5 minutes, then fluff it up with a fork before serving.

# THAI LARDER

In Bangkok, every part of the city has its own food market. These lively, bustling, social centres are the places to buy everything from fresh fruit, vegetables, meat, seafood and herbs to spices, sauces, relishes, pickles and ready-made curry pastes. And not forgetting the rows and rows of sweet bites that turn market stalls into veritable rainbows of colour. Of course, in the smaller cities, towns and villages throughout Thailand, markets are equally vital and food is brought in fresh in the morning to be sold that day.

The following ingredients are frequently used in Thai cooking and all feature within the recipes in this book. While many of them – lemongrass, Thai chillies, fresh kaffir lime leaves and galangal root to name a few – were perhaps unfamiliar to us in the West a few years ago, most are now readily available in supermarkets, Asian or oriental grocers, or online. All of the recipes in this book have been tested using widely found ingredients and, in the case of anything obscure, we've given familiar alternatives wherever possible.

## AUBERGINE

From elongated deep purple aubergines to white globes and green spherical balls, the Thais use an impressive selection of aubergines in their cooking in a spectrum of sizes and colours. Tiny pea aubergines, which are about the size of a small marble, and the slightly larger Thai aubergines (both are used in the recipe on page 116) can be eaten raw or cooked in curries. Even when cooked, pea aubergines, in particular, remain quite firm and have a slightly bitter flavour.

## BANANA LEAVES

The Asian equivalent to kitchen foil, these large, distinctive leaves are used to wrap foods ready to be steamed or char-grilled, but, unlike foil, the leaves also add flavour to what's inside the parcel. Softer young leaves are preferable as they are easier to fold than stiff, older ones, but if the latter is all you can find, remove the hard central stem and blanch the leaves before use. You'll usually find banana leaves in the freezer cabinet in Asian grocers – simply defrost before use.

## BASIL

Thai cooking uses various types of basil and they taste quite different to the regular basil we are familiar with in the West. Thai or sweet basil has deep green leaves that look a bit like mint, purplish buds, and stems with a lightly aniseed, liquorice flavour. The second type, holy basil, has narrower, darker green or purple leaves and deep purplish stems. It has a slight hint of cloves and is both sharp and hot in flavour.

## CHILLI

Chillies play a vital part in Thai cooking, providing colour, flavour and heat to all kinds of dishes, from snacks and appetizers to stir-fries and curries.

In this book, we've chosen to use just three types: small hot Thai chillies (bird's eye); medium-hot red/green chillies; and medium-hot long dried chillies. In true Thai-style, the seeds are generally left in, but for a milder alternative do remove them. Most chillies start off green and then turn red as they ripen, but both types usually have similar levels of heat and will keep in the fridge for a few days. Dried chillies are more convenient and will keep for much longer than fresh. We buy them in large bags – we use over 1 million chillies every year – to use in our curry pastes (see pages 254–6).

## COCONUT

Coconut is such a versatile ingredient and is used in various guises all over Southeast Asia – and Thailand is no exception. For the sake of convenience, we have used canned coconut milk in our recipes, yet Thais favour making their own using shredded or desiccated fresh coconut. It isn't difficult to make coconut milk, but it takes a little time and, when time-poor, canned coconut makes a welcome convenience. Rich and silky, coconut milk adds both texture and flavour to sweet and savoury dishes.

The coconut cream that forms on the top of the milk in the can makes a perfect non-dairy alternative to double cream – a quick tip, if it is very thin, put the can in the fridge to encourage the cream to rise to the surface. When making coconut-milk-based curries, it is usual to first 'cook' the curry paste in a small amount of coconut cream before adding the other ingredients. This helps to release the flavour of the dried spices in the paste as well as help the cream lose its 'rawness'.

Creamed coconut is the firm white block that you find in small cardboard packs and is not the same as coconut cream. It has a tendency to curdle, so we don't recommend it for use during cooking, but you can add it at the end to thicken or add a rich coconut flavour to a dish.

Desiccated coconut is dried, flaked or shredded and, as mentioned above, you can soak and blend it to make coconut milk, or sprinkle it, toasted or untoasted, over sweetmeats, desserts and savoury dishes. Look for the unsweetened variety.

## CORIANDER

Leaves, stalks and even coriander roots feature in Thai food – nothing goes to waste. The leaves are used both as part of a dish and as a garnish, scattered over the top before serving, while the stalks and roots add flavour to pastes and cooked dishes. Often the coriander on sale in Western supermarkets is sold in small packs and without its roots. Check out Asian grocers or independent food stores and you are likely to find large bunches with the roots intact, which are better value, too. Simply wash the roots to remove any dirt and then dry them with kitchen paper; they also freeze well if wrapped in a freezer-proof bag.

## FERMENTED YELLOW BEANS/PASTE/SAUCE

These salted yellow soya beans are sold whole or crushed as a thick paste or sauce and add an intense, robust flavour to stir-fries, marinades and braises. Salted black beans/paste/sauce are similar, but are made from black soya beans.

## FISH SAUCE

Don't be put off by its pungent aroma, fish sauce (*nam pla*) is synonymous with Thai food and is widely used as a flavouring in cooked dishes as well as fresh dipping sauces. The quality varies incredibly, so look for a brand that uses real seafood, rather than artificial flavourings. Made by curing anchovies or prawns in salt, fish sauce is not surprisingly both salty and fishy, yet it has the ability, if used in the right quantity, to lift and accentuate the flavours of a whole dish – magically, without overpowering them.

## GALANGAL (KHA)

A member of the ginger family, fresh galangal can be found in most Asian grocers, and some supermarkets now stock it. Although both rhizomes come from the same family, their flavour and appearance are quite different: galangal has aromatic almost citrus-cum-pine notes, while ginger is warmer and spicier – that said, they are sometimes used interchangeably. Visually, galangal is lighter in colour with a thin, smooth skin and a texture that is harder and drier than fresh ginger.

## GINGER

With its warm, spicy, lemony, peppery flavour, fresh ginger enhances the taste and aroma of sweet and savoury food. Pounded into fresh curry pastes, cut into matchsticks and added to stir-fries, grated into zingy marinades, or squeezed to extract the juice, there are many ways to use fresh ginger in Thai cooking. When shopping, look for plump, unwrinkled roots and store them wrapped in the fridge to keep them fresh. The easiest way to peel the root is to scrape it with the side of a teaspoon.

## KAFFIR LIME LEAVES

For the best flavour try to use fresh leaves, rather than dried or frozen – although the latter are preferable if fresh are out of the question. The leaves, from a citrus fruit of the same name, are dark green and glossy with a distinctive hour-glass shape and a unique fragrant lemon–lime flavour. Use them whole, shredded or torn to lift the flavour of curries, soups, broths, stir-fries, dressings and even desserts. The whole kaffir lime fruit is more tricky to find in the West and looks rather like a knobbly lime. Thais tend to use only the finely grated or pared zest in their cooking, rather than the juice of the fruit.

### KRACHAI

Like galangal, krachai is part of the ginger family and you'll likely find it in Asian grocers. Also known as 'lesser ginger', krachai looks like a cluster of small finger-shaped roots and lends an earthy, piquant note to dishes. Some recommend using fresh ginger as an alternative, but the two rhizomes really do taste quite different from one another and we would argue there is no real alternative to the real thing. You can also buy the root in powdered form.

### LEMONGRASS

It wasn't many years ago that lemongrass was difficult to find in Western food shops, but now the dried, thick, grass-like sticks are not an unfamiliar sight in most supermarkets – although we would maintain the best-quality ones are still to be found in Asian stores. Lemongrass lends an unmissably distinctive aroma to Thai food, while the sweet–sour, citrussy flavour lifts both sweet and savoury dishes. There are a few ways you can use it: bruised or crushed with the flat blade of a knife; pounded or blitzed into pastes for curry, soups and marinades; and finely chopped into dressings, relishes or stir-fries. It is usual to remove the tough, fibrous outer layer of the stick first, as the tender inner part is where the flavour lies. Lemongrass will keep wrapped in the fridge for up to 2 to 3 weeks.

### MANGO

Luscious and sweet, this golden-fleshed fruit is popular in desserts, relishes, sweetmeats, fresh juices, and lassis. In Thailand we also pickle mango. Under-ripe (green) mango is a familiar part of Thai salads and relishes, when it is shredded or sliced into fine strips to give a crisp, tart contrast to the rest of the ingredients. We have a tradition of using unripe fruit in Thai cooking: green papaya, for example, is used in much the same way as the mango – shredded into relishes and salads, such as the famous *som tam* (see page 202).

### MIANG LEAVES

These dark green, heart-shaped leaves, also known as wild betel leaves, could be described as edible wrappers, for that is how they are most commonly used. They are the base of the traditional Thai snack *miang kham* – meaning 'one-bite wrap'. In this dish, the leaf is topped with a taste-bud-tingling combination of hot, spicy, crunchy, sour and sweet ingredients, typically chillies, ginger, peanuts, coconut and dried shrimp (see page 240 for our version). In Thailand, the topped leaves are then arranged together on a large platter for everyone to help themselves, or in some restaurants and bars they are balanced on the top of a shot glass to be folded and popped in the mouth. The leaves don't need to be cooked and have a spicy, slightly bitter flavour, but if you can't find them in Asian grocers, it is possible to use crisp lettuce leaves, spinach leaves, steamed cabbage leaves, or chicory leaves instead – although none of these has quite the same visual appeal.

### MORNING GLORY (WATER MORNING GLORY)

This is a popular vegetable in Thailand and has long, jointed stems and arrow-shaped leaves. If you can't find it in Asian grocers, fresh spinach makes a suitable alternative.

### NOODLES

Noodles are the Thais second-most favourite carb – after rice, that is. There are many types to choose from, but most popular are cellophane noodles (glass or bean threads), which look similar to rice noodles and are made from mung beans; egg noodles, made with wheat and coloured with egg; and rice noodles, which are made from a simple paste of rice flour and water and are sold in varying widths. All are sold fresh, cooked or dried.

The thinnest noodles, vermicelli, are popular in rice paper rolls, soups and salads. They simply need soaking in hot water until just tender, then drained and dunked in a bowl of cold water until cool to stop them sticking together in a clump. Similarly, bean thread noodles are used in spring rolls or added to soups and are prepared in the same way. Rice ribbon noodles, or rice sticks, are flat and come in varying widths. Soak or cook these in boiling water and use them in stir-fries, coconut-based soups, and clear broths. A large bowl of steaming stir-fried noodles is one of our go-to lunches on our research trips to Bangkok's street-food markets.

### OYSTER SAUCE
Look for a good-quality brand that contains oyster extract – it should be top in the list of ingredients on the bottle – as cheaper products often contain very little, if any, oyster and are made up of artificial colours and other additives. This thick, dark brown sauce is popularly used to flavour meat, seafood and vegetable dishes.

### PALM SUGAR
Made from the juice of the coconut palm flower, palm sugar (also known as jaggery) is dark brown in colour with a rich, deep flavour – and unlike most other sugars, it has some nutritional value, too. Sold in solid blocks, ready to be grated or crumbled and then dissolved in liquid, or in a large crystallized form, it is often used to counterbalance any sour or bitter notes in a dish, including curries, sauces, dressings and marinades. If you have trouble finding it, soft dark or light brown sugar are suitable alternatives.

### PANDAN
According to Nigella Lawson, pandan (also known as *Pandanus* or screwpine) leaves are the next big food trend in the West, yet in Thailand they have been used for years as a wrapper or to add a vivid green colour as well as flavour to sweet and savoury food. Called the 'vanilla of Asia', the leaves are aromatic and, true to their name, have a distinct vanilla-like flavour. Packets of pandan leaves, chilled or frozen, are now fairly easy to find in Asian food stores.

### PEANUTS
Sprinkled over stir-fries and salads, served as a snack, or used as the base of satay sauce, peanuts (groundnuts) are widely used in Thai cooking. It is best to buy roasted unsalted peanuts or, better still, roast them yourself in a medium oven or in a large, dry frying pan or wok until light golden and aromatic; take care not to burn them, though, as they turn bitter. Groundnut oil is popular in Thai cooking, and features in recipes in the book, but in the restaurants we tend to use vegetable oil out of respect for guests who are allergic to peanuts.

### POMELO
With its rose-pink flesh and vibrant thick yellow/green skin, the pomelo is like a giant grapefruit, but with a drier texture. Its flavour marries grapefruit, orange and lemon and it is a popular addition to both sweet and savoury salads (see page 200).

### RICE
A staple food in Thailand, rice lies at the heart of most family meals. The most popular type of rice is jasmine, also known as fragrant rice. This long-grain variety (albeit shorter and thicker than Indian

basmati) has a slightly sticky texture and aromatic flavour that's great for soaking up sauces and curries and the perfect foil to hot, spicy food. Perhaps surprisingly, not all rice is the same and, as with most cooking ingredients, it pays to buy the best brand of rice you can afford – a good-quality jasmine rice will reward you with its wonderful fragrance and flavour.

Look out, too, for brown jasmine rice in Asian grocers, as it's nutritionally superior to white and has a lovely nutty flavour. Red rice is the latest thing, according to Bangkok foodies, and this ancient grain has a nutty flavour, and crisp texture.

If you are a big rice eater, it may pay to invest in a rice cooker, which 'guarantees' you perfectly cooked rice every time (many double as a slow cooker). Alternatively, follow the recipe for Perfect Jasmine Rice on page 259.

Sticky or glutinous white or black rice is entirely different to jasmine and, as its name suggests, has a much stickier texture. It is often eaten with the fingers during savoury parts of the meal, but is mainly used in Thai desserts and sweetmeats, including delicious coconut rice puddings. Our recipe (see page 225) uses black sticky rice, which contrasts so beautifully with the white of the coconut milk and the golden colour of the mango topping.

### SHRIMP PASTE (KAPI)
Extremely pungent, shrimp paste nevertheless has an amazing ability to lift and transform a dish if used in the right amount. An essential part of Southeast Asian cooking, and Thai food is no exception, the paste gives a salty, slightly fishy flavour to everything from stir-fries and curries to relishes and sauces. Before adding to a dish, it is usual to fry the paste

in a little oil or wrap it in a banana leaf or foil and roast or grill it for a couple of minutes to release its flavours. The paste will keep for ages stored chilled, but make sure you wrap it well to avoid its distinctive smell overwhelming your fridge. You'll find it in Asian grocers and some large supermarkets as a hard block or in a plastic tub or glass jar.

### SNAKE BEANS
This evocatively named bean, also known as yard-long bean, is (surprise, surprise) called after its long length. You should be able to snap the beans with your fingers (a sign of freshness) – any limp or soft beans are definitely past their best. If you can't find snake beans, equally fresh thin green or French beans are a suitable alternative.

### SOY SAUCE
Widely used in Thai cooking, but in more Chinese-style dishes, this sauce is made from fermented soya beans and comes in light and dark. Light is most popular and is thinner in consistency and saltier in flavour, while dark soy is thicker and sweeter – although still pretty salty. Both are strong-tasting so should be used carefully. If you are cooking for someone who is gluten-free, soy sauce without gluten is now widely available and makes for a straightforward recipe substitution.

### TAMARIND
This thick, sticky pulp adds a distinctive sourness to everything from curries and stir-fries to relishes and sauces, and is often used to counterbalance the sweetness of a dish. The dark brown pulp comes from the pods of the impressive-looking tamarind tree – many Thais have one in their garden, even in the cities. While it is possible to buy the pods, it's more usual to buy tamarind in a processed form. It comes as a dark, sticky block, which first needs

diluting in water and the seeds picked out, or as a concentrate or paste. The latter are most convenient and are used in the recipes in this book, as they don't need any preparation. However, shop-bought tamarind concentrate or paste can vary in quality, so look for brands that list tamarind at the top of the ingredients' label and those that contain a minimum of additives.

## WRAPPERS

Depending on whether a recipe calls for you to soak, steam or fry your dumpling, wonton or roll, it's important to choose the right type of wrapper for the job. Here is our handy guide to help you make the right decisions:

**Rice paper rolls** are traditionally made with dried rice paper wrappers. These fragile paper-thin round sheets should first be dunked briefly in hot water and then, when soft and slightly sticky, are ready for filling with noodles, vegetables, meat, seafood, herbs and really whatever you fancy. Once rolled, they will keep for an hour or so, but are best eaten straightaway with a dipping sauce.

**Spring roll wrappers** are thicker than rice paper wrappers and are usually sold chilled or frozen (defrost frozen wrappers before you use them). They come in rounds or squares that are suitable for shallow or deep-frying, and you can safely freeze – or refreeze – any that you don't use. The wrappers have a tendency to dry out when you open the pack, so fill one roll at a time, leaving the remainder covered with a damp clean tea towel.

**Wonton wrappers** are similar to spring roll wrappers, but tend to be thinner in texture. Like spring roll wrappers, they have a tendency to dry out once opened, so do keep them covered with a damp cloth. There are different types of wonton wrappers for steamed or fried dumplings, so do make sure you buy the right wrapper for the food you're making.

# INDEX

# ACKNOWLEDGEMENTS

We would like to thank Chef Jude Krit Sangsida who has spent hours in the kitchen, developing recipes along with his colleagues Tamas Khan and Benjarnan Nuanyai for this book. Jude started working at Busaba Bloomsbury as head chef in 2002 and became our executive chef in 2006. He has not only contributed with his delicious dishes but his kind soul and inspiration has been one of the supporting pillars of Busaba for years. We'd also like to thank our Head of Procurement, Winston Matthews, and Nicola Graimes, both of whom have helped to compile, write and test our recipes, for their insight, and for helping us to deliver our vision for Busaba's Thai cuisine.